Malcolm X

"I Believe in the Brotherhood of Man, All Men"

Read about other
American REBELS

Andy Warhol
"Everyone Will be Famous for 15 Minutes"

ISBN-13: 978-0-7660-3385-6

John Lennon
"Imagine"

ISBN-13: 978-0-7660-3675-8

Elvis Presley
"I Want to Entertain People"

ISBN-13: 978-0-7660-3382-5

Johnny Cash
"The Man in Black"

ISBN-13: 978-0-7660-3386-3

James Dean
"Dream As If You'll Live Forever"

ISBN-10: 0-7660-2537-3

Kurt Cobain
"Oh Well, Whatever, Nevermind"

ISBN-10: 0-7660-2426-1

Jimi Hendrix
"Kiss The Sky"

ISBN-10: 0-7660-2449-0

Madonna
"Express Yourself"

ISBN-10: 0-7660-2442-3

Malcolm X
"I Believe in the Brotherhood of Man, All Men"

ISBN-13: 978-0-7660-3384-9

Malcolm X

" I Believe in the Brotherhood of Man, All Men "

Jeff Burlingame

Enslow Publishers, Inc.
40 Industrial Road
Box 398
Berkeley Heights, NJ 07922
USA

http://www.enslow.com

Library of Congress Cataloging-in-Publication Data

Burlingame, Jeff.
    Malcolm X : "I believe in the brotherhood of man, all men" / Jeff Burlingame.
       p. cm. — (American rebels)
    Includes bibliographical references and index.
    Summary: "A biography of human rights activist Malcolm X, discussing his early struggles with racism, rise to fame as the public face of the Nation of Islam, personal hardships, and legacy"— Provided by publisher.
    ISBN 978-0-7660-3384-9
    1. X, Malcolm, 1925-1965—Juvenile literature. 2. African American Muslims—Biography— Juvenile literature. 3. African Americans—Race identity—Juvenile literature. 4. Race awareness— United States—Juvenile literature. 5. Afrocentrism—Juvenile literature. I. Title.
    BP223.Z8L57244 2010
    320.54'6092—dc22
    [B]
    9586   2009017597

Printed in the United States of America

052010 Lake Book Manufacturing, Inc., Melrose Park, IL

10 9 8 7 6 5 4 3 2 1

To Our Readers: This book has not been authorized by Malcolm X's estate or its successors.

We have done our best to make sure all Internet Addresses in this book were active and appropriate when we went to press. However, the author and the publisher have no control over and assume no liability for the material available on those Internet sites or on other Web sites they may link to. Any comments or suggestions can be sent by e-mail to comments@enslow.com or to the address on the back cover.

Every effort has been made to locate all copyright holders of material used in this book. If any errors or omissions have occurred, corrections will be made in future editions of this book.

♻ Enslow Publishers, Inc., is committed to printing our books on recycled paper. The paper in every book contains 10% to 30% post-consumer waste (PCW). The cover board on the outside of each book contains 100% PCW. Our goal is to do our part to help young people and the environment too!

Illustration Credits: Associated Press, pp. 64, 68, 74, 91, 93, 96, 123; Rebecca Cook/ Reuters/Landov, p. 135; Courtesy Archives of Michigan, p. 9; Everett Collection, Inc., pp. 39, 111, 119, 133; © First Run Features/courtesy Everett Collection, p. 80; Franklin Delano Roosevelt Presidential Library, p. 22; Library of Congress, Prints and Photographs Division, pp. 6, 15, 17, 117, 136; Rue des Archives/The Granger Collection, New York, p. 32; Shutterstock, p. 103; © SV-Bilderdienst/The Image Works, p. 70; © Topham/The Image Works, pp. 12, 28; © Tom Wirt, p. 24.

Cover Illustration: Time & Life Pictures/Getty Images (colored portrait).

Contents

Malcolm X in 1964.

Chapter 1

A Vivid Memory

The orange glow of the flames surrounded him. The smoke was so thick that it clogged his lungs. Malcolm Little could scarcely see or breathe, but he still could hear: the gunshots, the angry shouts of his father, and the terrifying screams of the rest of his family. It was those chaotic sounds that had roused him from his sleep, and those of the lifesaving family members who had rushed him outside before the fire had a chance to take his life, just four short years after it had begun.

Outside, in the middle of the chilly autumn darkness in Lansing, Michigan, Malcolm's family huddled together and watched as their home burned. Inside, the sound of an explosion cut through the flames. The farmhouse was destroyed. Malcolm later described what he recalled of the incident. He said, "We were lunging and bumping and tumbling all over each other trying to escape. My mother, with the baby in her arms, just made it into the yard before the house crashed in, showering sparks.

I remember we were outside in the night in our underwear, crying and yelling our heads off."[1]

Though it was one of his earliest memories, the destruction Malcolm saw on November 7, 1929, haunted him the rest of his life. He often talked about the event. In his autobiography, Malcolm discussed the fire—and whom he believed had caused it—in more detail. He wrote: "I remember being suddenly snatched awake into a frightening confusion of pistol shots and shouting and smoke and flames. My father had shouted and shot at the two white men who had set the fire and were running away."[2]

Malcolm's version of what happened next has been disputed over the years. As Malcolm told it, "[W]hite police and firemen came and stood around watching as the house burned down to the ground."[3] Others say the firefighters refused to come to help put out the blaze because the house was outside their jurisdiction and therefore not their fire to fight.[4] But by everyone's account, Malcolm's contention that the police were not completely helpful to his family was correct. In fact, when officers arrived on the scene, they arrested Malcolm's father, Earl Little, for illegal possession of a gun and suspicion of arson. They believed the father had intentionally set his own house on fire.[5]

Earl Little did have what could have been interpreted as a motive for setting the fire. Shortly before his house burned to the ground, he had been told that his family would have to move. Several of his white neighbors were against having a black family living in their neighborhood.

Lansing, Michigan, in the 1920s.

To get them to leave, they had argued that Little's purchase of the house had been illegal. They pointed to the home's deed, which read: "This land shall never be rented, leased, sold to, or occupied by . . . persons other than those of the Caucasian race."[6]

At the time, many facets of life in the United States were subject to racial segregation. Frequently, African Americans were not allowed to attend certain schools, eat at certain restaurants, or, as in this case, live in certain neighborhoods. Those living in Lansing's all-white community especially did not want a black family that was led by a person as controversial as Little in their neighborhood.

Life's lessons turned Malcolm Little into Malcolm X.

Little, a Baptist minister, was an outspoken and controversial man. He was a devotee of another black man, Marcus Garvey, who was the head of the Universal Negro Improvement Association (UNIA), a movement that called upon blacks to be proud of their heritage and to become independent from whites. Although slavery had been abolished in the United States several decades earlier, Garvey and his followers believed that in many ways, blacks still were enslaved to white people. He also felt that blacks never would be treated equally in America, so they should come together and return to Africa, which he believed to be their homeland. Little was one of Garvey's biggest supporters. This made him a target of white supremacist groups, such as the Ku Klux Klan. Whites saw Little as a troublemaker and frequently harassed him.

According to Malcolm, the fire was not the first time angry whites had seriously attacked his family. Most of the time, his defiant father stood up against his harassers and fought back. This time, there would be no fighting back. The house was destroyed, and the Little family had to salvage whatever belongings they could from the charred remains and find a new place to live.

Malcolm would later recall the fire as his first "vivid memory."[7] Unfortunately, life had several more traumatic times left for him to experience. When they happened, Malcolm internalized every moment of despair and every tragic circumstance. He gathered ideas from his father, from Garvey, and from the many other outspoken black men he would meet along the way. Life's lessons turned Malcolm Little into a controversial, defiant, and rebellious man with strong opinions as to the way black people should act. He had equally strong opinions of the white man who he felt held black people down. Life's lessons turned Malcolm Little into Malcolm X. There would come a time when everyone in the United States would know—many, even fear—that name.

Malcolm X addresses the crowd at a rally in Harlem, New York, in 1963.

Chapter 2

Tragic Beginnings

The world Malcolm Little was born into on May 19, 1925, was filled with anger and violence. Much of it came from his parents, Earl and Louise, who would fight over many issues, both large and small. Oftentimes the arguments were over a job—specifically, Earl Little's inability to find a steady one. By trade, he was a laborer, though he was frequently unemployed. By passion, he was a preacher and spent many of his waking hours practicing the craft. But that passion did not put food on the family table, nor did it pay the bills. Married six years by the time Malcolm was born, Earl and Louise Little fought so much that they often seemed more like enemies than husband and wife. Their dissimilar backgrounds may have had a lot to do with their fights.

Earl Little was poorly educated and spent most of his life doing manual labor. He also followed—and later taught—the beliefs of Marcus Garvey. Born in Jamaica, Garvey was a charismatic leader who believed blacks should unite and return to their homeland of Africa, where they could rule their own nation without the influence of oppressive whites. Garvey even created a fleet of freight ships called the Black Star Line to help transport black people to Africa. Garvey's speeches helped feed into the resentment many blacks in the United States had for white men. He even started his own militia.

Earl Little was president of the Omaha, Nebraska, branch of the UNIA. When Malcolm was born, Garvey was no longer leading the UNIA because he recently had been placed in prison for mail fraud. Little had desperately tried to get Garvey released from jail and had sent several letters asking for Garvey's release. He even sent one, dated June 8, 1927, to the president of the United States, Calvin Coolidge. The letter asked President Coolidge to "release Marcus Garvey from the five-year sentence without deportation which shall be your priceless gift to the Negro people of the world thus causing your name to be honored with generations yet unborn."[1] None of Little's efforts helped. Garvey soon was deported back to his home country of Jamaica. Even so, Little continued to preach Garvey's controversial message, and he traveled to various cities to spread word about the UNIA to other blacks.

Malcolm's mother was a follower of Garvey as well and believed in fighting for the rights of blacks. However, in nearly every other respect she was the opposite of her husband. Louise Little was raised on the Caribbean island of Grenada and had a high-school education, which made her one of the better-educated black women of her day. She had a black mother and a white father, which had left her with a light skin tone that often led people to believe she was white. She met Earl Little in Montreal, Canada, and the couple married in 1919. It was Earl Little's second marriage. His first one ended in divorce after he walked out on his wife and their three children.[2]

Marcus Garvey

Malcolm was his father's seventh child, and his mother's fourth. Like his mother, Malcolm also was born with light skin. His parents sometimes favored him over his older siblings—which included brothers Wilfred and Philbert and sister Hilda—because of this, but that did not mean Malcolm was treated well. The opposite was true, in fact. Sometimes his mother would scrub his skin with a brush to try to make it even lighter. She once told a white neighbor, "I can make him look almost white if I bathe him enough."[3] Other times, his conflicted mother would send Malcolm outside to play in the sun to make his skin darker.

Then there were the beatings. Malcolm seemed to get less of them from his father than his siblings and his mother did, but he still got them. A majority of the time, when Malcolm was whipped, it came from his mother, who herself had been abused as a child.

The turmoil in young Malcolm's life not only came from inside his home. It came from outside it, too. Because of his beliefs and his outspoken personality, Earl Little was the target of many white supremacists, who believed he was nothing but a troublemaker. One often-repeated story says that while Malcolm was still in his mother's womb, his family's home was surrounded by several members of the Ku Klux Klan, who were wearing hoods, riding horses, and carrying guns. They were looking for Earl Little. Malcolm later described the event in his autobiography. He wrote:

> My mother went to the front door and opened it. Standing where they could see her pregnant condition, she told them that she was alone with her three small children, and that my father was away, preaching, in Milwaukee. The Klansmen shouted threats and warnings that we had better get out of town because "the good Christian white people" were not going to stand for my father's "spreading trouble" among the "good" Negroes of Omaha with the "back to Africa" preachings of Marcus Garvey.[4]

A clause in the deed to the Littles' home stated that no blacks could live on the property.

Malcolm also said the Klansmen shattered every window in his family's house and then rode off into the night. Some family members, including Malcolm's mother, have said they doubt that incident even happened.[5]

Whether or not the story was true, the Littles did leave Omaha soon after Malcolm was born. They briefly lived in Milwaukee, Wisconsin, and Albion, Michigan, before settling into an old, two-story farmhouse on the outskirts of Lansing, Michigan. Earl Little hoped he finally had found a place where his family might be safe from the persecution they had received because of the color of their skin. It did not happen that way. The section of Lansing the Littles moved into was primarily white, and Earl Little continued to speak out for black empowerment and independence. Those two factors were not a good combination, and they kept the peaceful life he desired out of Earl Little's reach.

When Malcolm was four years old, a group of white neighbors found a legal means to get the Littles to move. A clause in the deed to

Klansmen like these terrorized the Little family.

the Littles' home stated that no blacks could live on the property. The neighbors went to court to sue the Littles and won, forcing them to move. But Earl Little was defiant. He was determined to remain in the house he had bought and, not surprisingly, was willing to fight for it.

That turned out to be a bad decision. Two weeks after the court judgment, on November 7, 1929, the house caught fire in the middle of the night while the family was asleep, and it burned to the ground. Fortunately, the family escaped before anyone was injured. Malcolm and many other historians blame a white supremacist group for starting the fire. However, authorities at the scene arrested Earl Little, thinking he may have deliberately set the blaze with the theory that if he could not have the house, then no one could. Charges against Little were later dropped.[6]

Their home in ruins, the Littles were forced to move again. They eventually wound up a short distance away in East Lansing, Michigan. Thanks to donations from others, Earl Little was able to raise money to purchase six acres of farmland there, and he built a four-room house on the property. It sounds like a comfortable living situation, but actually it was not. The rural home did not have indoor plumbing and was poorly insulated, offering little protection from the chilly Michigan winters. However, it was home to Malcolm and his family. They made do with what they had. They used the large amount of land around them to raise their own food. They had chickens and rabbits and grew vegetables in their garden.

There were seven children living in the Little household in 1931, the year Malcolm began kindergarten at Pleasant Grove Elementary School. And although he and his siblings were the only black children in the school, all indications are that they were treated well by their classmates. For a short time, the rural setting allowed the Littles to escape persecution from bigoted white people and live in a peaceful manner. But the violence that had plagued the family soon continued.

> **Malcolm was a few months into his sixth year, when the worst tragedy yet struck his family.**

Malcolm was a few months into his sixth year when the worst tragedy yet struck his family. On September 28, 1931, his father was found dying on some streetcar tracks in Lansing. Officials determined Earl Little had been accidentally run over by a streetcar. A newspaper account of his death reported the same thing. It read:

> The car was operated by William Hart, 1417 Vine Street, who told Coroner Ray Gorsline that he did not see the man before the accident. It is believed that he fell under the rear trucks as he was running for the car. Coroner Gorsline found that Little had taken another car which passed about 12 minutes before the car operated by Hart. He reached for his pocket when he boarded it, but told the motorman to let him off at the next corner. He did not have an overcoat on at this time, it

was said, but did have an overcoat on when the accident occurred. It is believed that he discovered that he had forgotten his coat when he reached for his purse, and that he got off the car to go back for it. The coroner has been unable to discover he left the coat. When he was found his purse and a street car check were in the overcoat pocket.[7]

In spite of the reports, some blacks believed Earl Little was attacked and brutally beaten by the Black Legionnaires hate group, and then his body was placed on the tracks where the streetcar eventually ran him over. Malcolm also believed this version of the story. He had gone to many meetings with his father, had heard him preach the gospel of Garvey, and had seen the disdain many white folks had for Garvey, his father, and any black man who spoke out for equality. Whatever happened to Earl Little, he was barely clinging to life when he was found and taken to the hospital. He died shortly after he arrived there.

Work was even harder to come by for blacks, especially black women with little or no work history.

Authorities woke Malcolm's family in the middle of the night to deliver the news. To any family, that type of news would have been destructive and upsetting. To the Littles, it was simply devastating. At the time, the United States was in the midst of the Great Depression, an era where work was difficult to come by and millions of people lost their jobs, homes, and savings because of it. For many people, finding a job during the Great Depression was nearly impossible.

Work was even harder to come by for blacks, especially black women with little or no work history. But that is what Louise Little now faced if she wanted to support her family. So, Louise found some odd jobs here and there. Her light skin helped her get cleaning jobs in homes of white people who might otherwise not have let her work for them. When she straightened her naturally curly hair, it was difficult for many people to tell she was black. But when her employers discovered she was black or that she was the widow of the outspoken Earl Little, they immediately fired her.

With each job loss, her children suffered. Malcolm's oldest brother, Wilfred, quit school and found odd jobs to help. Still, Malcolm and his siblings were forced to eat whatever they could. Often, that meant very little. The family took handouts from whoever offered them. Whatever money they could get, they would spread as far as they could, buying the cheapest ingredients and making them last. Malcolm recalled, "[T]here were times when there wasn't even a nickel and we would be so hungry and dizzy. My mother would boil a big pot of dandelion greens, and we would eat that. . . . [C]hildren would tease us, that we ate 'fried grass.'"[8] Despite the teasing, Malcolm remained a popular kid in school. Class photographs show a grinning boy who is a half head taller than the next-tallest boy in his class.

To survive, Louise Little eventually had to accept welfare benefits from the government. It was a terribly

The Great Depression

The Great Depression was a worldwide economic crisis that left millions of people unemployed, homeless, and starving. It began with the stock market crash of October 24, 1929, known as "Black Thursday," in the United States and spread to Europe and other industrialized nations. Farmers in the Midwest were hit especially hard. In the 1930s, drought and severe dust storms destroyed their lands, an event called the Dust Bowl. The farmers were forced to leave their homes in search of work elsewhere, but conditions in the rest of the country were no better. In 1932, Franklin D. Roosevelt was elected president and he introduced the New Deal, a series of government programs designed to relieve unemployment, to stimulate the economy, and to prevent such a devastating event from ever happening again. Although the New Deal did help, the Great Depression did not end until the 1940s, when the United States entered World War II.

During the Great Depression, many Americans had to depend on charity-run bread lines for food.

humiliating concession for the once-proud woman, and it took a toll on her mental health. She wanted to work and did not like taking handouts. So she began to withdraw from society and, as Malcolm put it, she would "talk to herself nearly all of the time now, and there was a crowd of new white people entering the picture—always asking questions. . . . Eventually my mother suffered a complete [mental] breakdown, and the court orders were finally signed. They took her to the State Mental Hospital in Kalamazoo."[9] This happened on January 9, 1939. Louise Little stayed there for the next twenty-six years.

By that point, the state already had declared Louise Little an unfit parent and had taken all but her oldest children away from her. Malcolm, now thirteen, was placed in the care of foster parents Mabel and Thornton Gohanna. The Gohannas were paid to take in problem children. That is exactly what Malcolm had become. The tall, thin teenager who once had excelled in sports—such as basketball, football, baseball, and even boxing—had taken to stealing food from the local store to help his family. He had been kicked out of school several times for misbehaving, although it was no surprise to anyone that he did so. He had lived a childhood that would be tough for anyone to come out of unscathed. His family had been attacked for the color of their skin. He had become sick from hunger. His father had died a tragic death. His mother had suffered a nervous breakdown. And those were just the major events Malcolm had endured.

This historical marker stands outside what was once the homesite of Malcolm X in Lansing, Michigan. The house no longer exists.

After his mother was sent to the mental institution, Malcolm left the Gohannas' house and returned to his home, where Wilfred and Hilda had been allowed to remain to take care of the family household. Both worked hard to do so, with Wilfred taking on the role of father and Hilda becoming the acting mother. Hilda also tried to stay in school and took miscellaneous jobs when she could to help pay the bills. She described one of her scary work environments in a letter to a family member. It read: "I had another job working for an old stingy couple. The woman was fussy and the man was off in the head. I thought maybe I could put up with it, but when the man came walking in the kitchen one day with a hammer and a butcher knife, it didn't take me long to quit. I haven't worked since."[10]

Despite his older siblings' valiant efforts to keep the house in order, Malcolm did not live there long this time. In the fall of 1939, the state sent him to a juvenile detention home in the small, nearby town of Mason, Michigan. The home was run by the Swerlein family. Malcolm liked the Swerleins and at the time thought the feeling was mutual, although he would later say the family only liked him "in the way they liked their house pets."[11]

Malcolm attended Mason Junior High School, where he became class president and received good grades—for a while, at least. As one of the only black students in a mostly white school, it was not long before he realized that being a black teen—even a *well-liked* black teen—would have its limitations. For example, it was

25

considered improper for black boys to date white girls, although several of them reportedly had a crush on the handsome Malcolm. But if Malcolm attempted to talk to a white girl, he would be browbeaten by the white boys watching it occur. Biographer Bruce Perry said Malcolm was the first person to be blamed when something was stolen at school, and he was not even allowed to get his hair cut in the town of Mason. Even the Swerleins called him names.

Malcolm was discouraged at how he was treated but tolerated it as well as could be expected. As much as one could, he was growing used to the abuse. Being treated differently from his white classmates made Malcolm long to find his place in the world. Did such a place even exist? He was talented in many ways, especially speaking, and one day he told an English teacher he would like to use that gift and become a lawyer to help down-and-out families like his. The teacher discouraged Malcolm from that career path. The teacher said, "We all here like you, you know that. But you've got to be realistic about being a nigger. A lawyer— that's no realistic goal for a nigger. You need to think about something you *can* be. . . . Why don't you plan on carpentry?"[12] The term *nigger* is a racial slur derived from the Latin word for black. It is extremely insulting to black people.

Years later, Malcolm mentioned that believing what

> **Soon, Malcolm's negative thoughts became a self-fulfilling prophecy.**

that teacher had told him was one of his biggest regrets in life. He said:

> My greatest lack has been, I believe, that I don't have the kind of academic education I wish I had been able to get—to have been a lawyer, perhaps. I do believe that I might have made a good lawyer. I have always loved verbal battle, and challenge. You can believe me that if I had the time right now, I would not be one bit ashamed to go back into any New York City public school and start where I left off at the ninth grade, and go on through a degree.[13]

The teacher's discouraging suggestion had a huge impact on Malcolm. Why should he study when he could not be what he wanted to be anyway? Furthermore, what was the point of even going to school when he could become a laborer without an education? Both were valid questions that Malcolm began to think about. Soon, Malcolm's negative thoughts became a self-fulfilling prophecy. He stopped focusing on his studies, and again he began to cause trouble at school.

It became apparent that Malcolm might need another change of scenery. Surely, there was some place in the world for an intelligent, yet misguided, black teenager who was at a pivotal stage in his development. When Malcolm was fifteen, he found one.

Malcolm X lectures students in London, England, on February 11, 1965.

Chapter 3

An Informal Education

Ella Collins was Malcolm's half sister, one of the three children Earl Little had fathered with his first wife. In 1941, Collins lived in Boston, Massachusetts, and, especially by Little family standards, she was doing remarkably well. She had married—and later divorced— a doctor and was well respected in the neighborhood she lived in.

Malcolm had first visited her in the summer of 1940, and he enjoyed his time in the big city. It was an exciting opportunity for the teen and his first chance to meet several of his father's relatives. After his visit, Malcolm returned to Michigan, went back to school for a short while, and then dropped out. What he planned to do next was anyone's guess, but a letter from Collins helped make his decision a lot easier. It read:

> Dear Malcolm . . . I don't know how to write to
> you. But I will try. . . . Sas lives in the mailbox
> looking for a letter from you. Gracie thought

maybe you would be back by now. I *know* better. I had one of those long nightmares & dreams about you last nite. In fact, every nite since you left. We miss you so much. . . . [E]verything seems dead here. . . . I would like for you to come back but under one condition—*Your mind is made up*.[1]

Collins wanted to make sure Malcolm was serious about staying with her before he made the decision to come back to Boston. She could not take becoming attached to him again only to have him leave once more. She loved her younger brother from the first time she met him when he was just six years old, at their father's funeral in 1931. She believed her little brother was unique. She said, "I knew he was a special child. He was lovable, smart, and quietly assertive."[2] The admiration was mutual. In his autobiography, Malcolm wrote about the first time he met his big sister: "[S]he was the first really proud black woman I had ever seen in my life. She was plainly proud of her very dark skin. This was unheard of among Negroes in those days, especially in Lansing. . . . The way she sat, moved, talked, did everything, bespoke somebody who did and got exactly what she wanted. . . . I had never been so impressed with anybody."[3]

Malcolm took his sister up on her offer to move to Boston. His decision to do so was celebrated at Collins's home. She said, "I thanked the spirits of John, our grandfather. I knew Malcolm had some doubts about moving in with us, doubts that were reinforced by meddling social workers and their divisive tactics."[4]

Malcolm and his sister lived in a mostly black, middle-class area of the city known by locals as "the Hill." The Hill was located next to Roxbury, the black ghetto section of Boston. The streets around Malcolm's new home were filled with black people; it was unlike anything Malcolm had seen before. All his life Malcolm had been surrounded by white people—from his schoolteachers and his classmates to the social workers that frequently came to check on his mother and the rest of his family. Now, there were so many people that looked just like him, mingling through the area with purpose and a sense of belonging— exactly what Malcolm wanted for himself. It did not take long for him to begin to feel comfortable in his new environment. But that familiarity did not come exactly the way his half sister had wanted it to. Collins had hoped Malcolm would hang in the Hill area, where the more-upstanding blacks lived. But Malcolm did not get along well with the people on the Hill. He believed they acted as if they were better than he was. So instead of hanging out on the Hill, Malcolm began venturing off to Roxbury.

> **The streets around Malcolm's new home were filled with black people; it was unlike anything Malcolm had seen before.**

The streets of Roxbury were filled with hustlers— people who would use any means necessary to acquire goods or money. They would gamble, steal, and deal drugs. Malcolm's formal education may have ended

The Savoy Ballroom in Harlem, like the Roseland State Ballroom in Roxbury, was a popular place where people would go to listen to music and to dance.

back in Michigan, but his street education began in Roxbury. The hustlers were his teachers.

Malcolm found a job shining shoes at Roxbury's trendy Roseland State Ballroom, where he met many famous musicians, such as Count Basie and Duke Ellington. When he was not working, Malcolm enjoyed the dancing the popular venue had to offer him. By most accounts, Malcolm was a talented dancer. Like many of Roxbury's blacks, Malcolm began wearing a flashy type of clothing called a zoot suit, which featured baggy, high-waisted pants that were pegged at the ankle, with a long jacket worn over the top of it all. He often wore a matching hat. Malcolm soon earned himself a nickname on the streets of Roxbury. He was called "Red," after his red-tinted hair, which he began to conk, or slick down with a substance called congolene.

Soon after he arrived in Boston, Malcolm began to hang out with "Shorty," a man whose real name was Malcolm Jarvis. Shorty also was from Lansing, and he became Malcolm's mentor on the streets of Roxbury. Soon, the two became partners in crime, hanging out in Roxbury's pool halls and dive bars. Just sixteen, Malcolm was too young to legally be allowed into the bars, but he was tall, sharply dressed, and looked much older than his age, so it was no problem for him to get in. Shorty and Malcolm also were drinking alcohol, gambling, smoking marijuana, and, soon, committing burglaries.

Collins was not pleased with her brother's actions. She had brought him from Michigan to Boston to free him from his life of poverty and to give him an opportunity to make something positive of his life. She spent a lot of time pushing him to become a better person and attempting to mold him into the successful black man she knew he could be. But it seemed as if all her efforts were wasted. Malcolm preferred hanging out with his friends in Roxbury rather than spending time with his family and the people in their higher-class neighborhood on the Hill. This is exactly what he did. His sister did not agree with his actions. She said, "I didn't admire his using that rebellious streak against himself by using drugs and throwing away his money on zoot suits and conked hair and against his own people by selling them drugs."[5]

Collins was furious when Malcolm eventually lost his shoe-shining job and began his life of illegal activity. She said, "As deeply hurt as I felt . . . I wasn't about to help him lead a life of destructive behavior."[6] Years later, Malcolm recognized his actions had let his sister down. He said, "Ella couldn't believe how atheist, how uncouth I had become. I believed that a man should do anything that he was slick enough, or bad and bold enough, to do and that a woman was nothing but another commodity."[7]

Collins did not give up hope for her younger brother. She helped to get Malcolm another job, as a soda jerk, someone who served ice cream, sodas, and more at a drugstore soda fountain. One of Malcolm's regular customers there was a black girl named Laura who lived across the street. She was a year older and a high-school honor student. Malcolm was attracted to her innocence, and the two teens soon became a couple. They would go dancing at the Roseland, and Malcolm even brought her home to meet his sister, who approved of her. Collins must have been disappointed, then, at the time when Malcolm took Laura home early after an evening of dancing at the Roseland so he could return to the ballroom to meet a different young woman, a well-dressed white girl named Beatrice. For a black man at the time, there was a certain coolness to be dating a white woman, and Malcolm showed Bea off every chance he got. As fast as she had come into Malcolm's life, Laura was out of it.

> **For a black man at the time, there was a certain coolness to be dating a white woman. Malcolm showed Bea off every chance he got.**

For various reasons, Collins did not like Bea. She wanted to get Malcolm away from his new girlfriend and away from the rest of the crowd they were running with. So she helped him get a job as a kitchen worker on a railroad. Malcolm did not want to do it at first but decided to take the job because it allowed him to travel to the biggest cities on the East Coast, including Washington, D.C.; Baltimore, Maryland; and Philadelphia, Pennsylvania. Malcolm also often made the four-hour trek to New York City. The stories he had heard of New York made it out to be an exciting, mythical, and near-magical place, and Malcolm wanted to see it. Though neither he nor his sister had any indication it might, Malcolm's railroad job caused even more problems for the sixteen-year-old.

Had Malcolm been a couple of years older, seeing New York City would not have been an option—at least not at that point in his life. That is because in December 1941, Japan's military bombed Pearl Harbor, Hawaii, and the United States entered World War II. Young men like Malcolm were drafted to help their country fight the war. But because he was only sixteen, Malcolm was not eligible to be drafted, and he was able to continue his mischievous ways. Not being eligible for the draft also likely allowed Malcolm to obtain his railroad job. Because so many men were now in the military, there were many job openings. Working on the railroad was considered a good job, and it is unlikely Malcolm could have gotten it if it were not wartime.

> **On his first visit there, Malcolm fell in love with New York.**

On his first visit there, Malcolm fell in love with New York. He was especially fond of the black area of the city, Harlem. Malcolm found Harlem similar to Boston's Roxbury district, only bigger and more exciting. Harlem was *alive*, full of black men and women participating in the many activities and events the area had to offer. The streets were full of blacks of all social classes. Down-on-their-luck prostitutes lived in Harlem. So did rich doctors. Malcolm was inspired by the latter fact, but he was also disappointed that, even in the 1940s, the well-off blacks were not allowed to live in some of the city's

Harlem Renaissance

The Harlem Renaissance was an African-American political, cultural, and intellectual movement that took place in the 1920s and 1930s. It began in Harlem, New York, but its ideas influenced communities throughout the United States and in other parts of the world. Politicians, philosophers, artists, writers, musicians, and others focused on issues affecting African Americans. They sought to obliterate the negative stereotypes and to promote civil rights.

Even after slavery was abolished, life in the South was still difficult for blacks. The Fourteenth Amendment made former slaves citizens of the United States. Therefore, African Americans should have had the same rights as white citizens. However, many Southern states were passing unfair laws to strip African Americans of their rights. They migrated to the North where there were more opportunities for economic and social advancement. They settled in places such as Harlem and Chicago and established their own schools, churches, and businesses. However, life up North was far from perfect. African Americans were still treated like second-class citizens and faced poverty and discrimination on a daily basis. They expressed their frustrations, shed light on the injustices, and sought to demonstrate their humanity through music, art, and literature. Jazz music became the sound track of the movement through such artists as Louis Armstrong, Billie Holiday, and Duke Ellington. Novels, drama, and poetry depicting black life gained popularity. Notable writers of the period include Langston Hughes, Zora Neale Hurston, and Claude McKay.

Although all the prominent figures of the Harlem Renaissance sought to advance African Americans, there were opposing views as to how to go about it. Marcus Garvey believed blacks would never obtain equality in America and that they should all settle in Africa. In contrast, W.E.B. DuBois thought integration was possible through education and political action. Malcolm X and Dr. Martin Luther King, Jr., echoed these opposing ideologies decades later. The Harlem Renaissance set the stage for the civil rights movement of the 1960s.

more upper-class neighborhoods. Malcolm was seeing firsthand what his father and Marcus Garvey had said: blacks often were treated as inferior by whites. Malcolm, in fact, believed the opposite to be true, that whites were the inferior species. He told one interviewer:

> Anyone who has studied the genetic phase of biology knows that white is considered recessive and black is considered dominant. When you want strong coffee, you ask for black coffee. If you want it light, you want it weak, integrated with white milk. . . . If you want bread with no nutritional value, you ask for white bread. All the good that was in it has been bleached out of it, and it will constipate you. If you want pure flour, you ask for dark flour. . . . If you want pure sugar, you ask for dark sugar.[8]

But that did not mean Malcolm thought blacks were perfect. He believed their biggest weakness came from trying to act white. He also told the same journalist:

> There is plenty wrong with Negroes. They have no society. They're robots, automations. No minds of their own. . . . They are a black body with a white brain. Like the monster Frankenstein. . . . At the bottom on the social heap is the black man in the big-city ghetto. He lives night and day with the rats and cockroaches and drowns himself with alcohol and anesthetize[s] himself with dope, to try and forget where and what he is. That Negro has given up all hope.[9]

Still, as an uneducated black man, it was not those professionals with whom Malcolm would associate when

Harlem, New York, in the 1940s.

he lost his train job, left his sister's house in Boston, and moved to Harlem in the spring of 1943. He was back hanging out with the same type of crowd he had before. He found a job as a waiter in a Harlem bar called Small's Paradise. Small's was a hot spot for well-dressed businessmen who liked to enjoy a cocktail or two after the workday was through. It also was a hot spot for first-rate hustlers and thugs, the likes of which Malcolm had never seen. If what he learned in Roxbury had been his high school, Harlem was his university. He would learn a lot there, especially from those who frequented or worked at Small's. Most of what he learned was not positive, including how to be paid to find prostitutes for the men who were looking for them. That led to his eventual firing from Small's when, one day, he agreed to find a prostitute for one of the bar's customers. It turned out that the customer was an undercover police officer. Malcolm was not arrested, but he did lose his job. Now, instead of simply supplementing his income with the petty crimes he was committing, those crimes soon became his only source of income—and the source of a lot more trouble.

On the streets of Harlem, Malcolm began going by the name "Detroit Red" to help distinguish him from the other "Reds" in the area. As he had done in Boston, Malcolm began selling drugs to his friends and acquaintances. The money he made from those illegal transactions paid for his own drug—and gambling— habits. Malcolm had been smoking marijuana and drinking alcohol for a while, but in Harlem he began using harder drugs, such as heroin and cocaine. He said he smoked marijuana, popularly known at the time as "reefer," day and night. He also said the cocaine gave him "an illusion of supreme well-being, and a soaring overconfidence in both physical and mental ability. You think you could whip the heavyweight champion, and that you are smarter than anybody."[10]

Even though Malcolm may have felt invincible, thanks in part to the drugs, he actually was anything but. His drug deals and robberies had left him somewhat paranoid, and he moved from motel to motel to keep from being caught by police. His paranoia was justified. Police were said to always be on the lookout for him, although Malcolm also said some of those police ignored his activity. He said, "I had a good working system of paying off policemen. . . . I had several men working and I was a steerer myself. I steered white people with money from downtown to whatever kind of sin they wanted in Harlem. I didn't care what they wanted, I knew where to take them to it. . . . [And] my best customers always were the officials, the top police people, businessmen, politicians and clergymen."[11]

> **Malcolm's feelings about white people changed throughout his life.**

Malcolm's feelings about white people changed throughout his life. In his youth, he had wanted to be white, as that was the only way he thought he could become successful in life. As he grew, he began to hate white people for the way he felt they treated blacks like

41

second-class citizens. He was not the only black person who felt that way. When Malcolm was coming of age, racial tensions were high across the entire United States. In areas where there were large numbers of blacks, such as Harlem, they were especially so.

Shortly after Malcolm arrived in Harlem, a white police officer shot and wounded a black soldier who reportedly had taken offense to the language the officer had used with a black woman he was arresting. False rumors quickly began to spread that the white cop had killed the black soldier. Thousands of blacks rioted in the streets, looting stores and other buildings. The military was called in to help the city's police force gain control, and fifteen hundred civilians were enlisted to help, as well. In the end, five people were killed, four hundred were injured, and five hundred people, all of them black, were arrested.[12]

> **When Malcolm was coming of age, racial tensions were high across the entire United States.**

Property damages were estimated at $5 million.[13] One report described the situation in detail: "Many of the rioters were in their late teens or early twenties, and some wore zoot suits. They appeared to be organized in gangs ranging in size up to forty or fifty persons, some of which included young girls and children. In some cases the girls and children followed the gangs and ran away with loot the older boys and men had thrown into the street."[14]

After Malcolm had committed a series of robberies

with his friend and accomplice Sammy McKnight, he sensed it was time for him to get out of town. He needed to get away for a while to take some of the heat off him. So he headed back to Boston, where he began hanging out with the same people he had been running with before he left. His old girlfriend, Bea, was now married to a man who was away in the military, but this did not stop Malcolm from seeing her again. He also reunited with his mentor, Shorty, and resumed his life of crime on the Boston streets.

Malcolm's half sister, Ella Collins, was not happy with any of it. Again, she felt upset that her brother had not taken her early advice and aid and used it to become a law-abiding citizen. She said, "I was extremely disappointed, hurt, and angry that my younger brother, who I knew was very intelligent, with great leadership potential, had fallen into the hoary trap of an affair with a white woman. It meant that he had accepted . . . that having a white woman was a much-desired status symbol."[15] Herself a strong and successful—and mostly calm—black woman, Collins even once resorted to violence. She said, "The whole situation enraged me so much that once, during an argument, I actually tried to throw both of them down a flight of stairs in the house as they were leaving."[16]

After Malcolm turned eighteen years old in 1943, he was afforded another opportunity to get off the streets and to begin living a lawful life. The United States Army, still in the midst of World War II, tried to bring him into its ranks. Malcolm did not want to go to war.

Long known by his peers as a joker, Malcolm devised a plan. On the day he was called into the army's recruiting office in Manhattan, he put on his zoot suit and his yellow shoes. From the moment he walked in the office, he began acting strange. When he was brought in to see the army psychiatrist, he continued his act. Constantly looking around the room as if he were paranoid about being spied on, Malcolm stood up from his seat and whispered in the doctor's ear: "Daddy-o, now you and me, we're from up North here, so don't you tell nobody. . . . I want to get sent down South. Organize them nigger soldiers, you dig? Steal us some guns, and kill us crackers!"[17]

Even though Malcolm's behavior was all an act to keep him out of the military, the army did just that. A report by the Federal Bureau of Investigation released years later stated the army's reasoning. It read: "[O]n October 25, 1943 the subject was found mentally disqualified for military service for the following reasons: psychopathic personality inadequate, sexual perversion, psychiatric rejection."[18] Thanks to some good acting, Malcolm was again free to work the streets—until the law finally caught up with him.

That happened in Boston in early 1946. In the city where his sister had brought him to help better his life, Malcolm had become the leader of a small burglary ring that included Shorty, Bea, and her sister. On January 12, Malcolm entered a jewelry story to pick up a stolen watch he had left there to be repaired. The store's owner was suspicious and summoned police, who arrived and arrested Malcolm on the spot. Malcolm surrendered willingly, and he was fully cooperative in the ensuing investigation. He told the arresting officer about the loaded gun he was carrying. When questioned about a string of burglaries the police believed he had been involved in, Malcolm admitted to all of them. He even ratted out his fellow conspirators. His goal was to receive a lighter sentence by being cooperative. It did not work out that way.

Malcolm's bail was set at ten thousand dollars, an amount far too steep for him to pay, so he had to remain in jail while he awaited trial, which was held in February. At the trial, the three white girls who had been arrested with Malcolm were seated at a table, while Malcolm and Shorty watched the proceedings from inside a locked cage. Malcolm had no lawyer, but he remained calm throughout the proceedings. In the

In the city where his sister had brought him to help better his life, Malcolm had become the leader of a small burglary ring.

end, he received a sentence of eight to ten years in prison. Many considered the sentence to be a steep one, considering the normal sentence for such crimes would be two or three years in prison. But Malcolm had a prior arrest, and the women involved in the robbery had said he forced them to participate. Shorty received the same sentence as Malcolm. Despite those factors, Malcolm felt he was treated unfairly because of his skin color and the fact that he was a black man who had been running around with white women. Malcolm said: "The social workers worked on us. White women in league with Negroes was their main obsession. The girls weren't so-called 'tramps,' or 'trash,' they were well-to-do upper-middle-class whites. That bothered the social workers. How, where, when, had I met them? Did we sleep together? Nobody wanted to know anything at all about the robberies. All they could see was that we had taken the white man's women."[19]

His observations led Malcolm to distrust even more the American justice system in general and the white people who ran it in particular. During his time in prison, that distrust would continue to grow.

Chapter 4

Falling for the Nation of Islam

Malcolm was almost twenty-one years old when he arrived at Boston's Charlestown State Prison in February 1946. No longer was he "Red," as he had been called on the streets of Roxbury. Neither was he "Detroit Red," as he had been known during his time in Harlem. In this dark place of confinement, Malcolm was now known by his prison number: 22483.

Having been built in 1805, Charlestown was the oldest state prison in Massachusetts, and it certainly showed its age. In fact, the prison had once been in such bad shape that it had been shut down, only to be reopened a short time later when another prison grew too crowded. Malcolm's cell was dirty and tiny, and it had no running water. His toilet was a bucket in the corner of the cell. Just as noteworthy, for Malcolm at least, was that the prison had no drugs, at least not the ones he was used to taking.

On the streets, Malcolm had become addicted to

cocaine. Without it, he was a cranky man, causing trouble almost from the moment he arrived at the prison. He was mean to everyone he encountered, including guards and fellow inmates. This earned him a lot of time in solitary confinement, where prisoners are separated from the rest of the population and placed in even-smaller cells than they had been in before. One of the reasons for solitary confinement is to leave troublemaking prisoners alone with their thoughts, in the hope that they will realize what they did wrong and behave better when they are placed back in with the general population.

Malcolm did not learn from his stint in solitary. He continued being belligerent, and he spoke so negatively about organized religion that people began calling him "Satan." Malcolm had been raised in a religious household, but during his time in Boston and Harlem, he had lost all connection to religion. If there was a god, where was he when Malcolm needed his help? Malcolm's answer was that he was not around. Malcolm became a nonbeliever and even made fun of those who did believe.

Malcolm obviously was not happy with his situation in life, and he was rebelling against everyone and everything because of it. No one was off limits, not even people who were trying to help him or to be friendly.

> **Malcolm obviously was not happy with his situation in life, and he was rebelling against everyone and everything because of it.**

Malcolm later wrote in his autobiography: "The prison psychologist interviewed me and he got called every filthy name I could think of, and the prison chaplain got called worse. My first letter, I remember, was from my religious brother Philbert in Detroit, telling me his 'holiness' church was going to pray for me. I scrawled him a reply I'm ashamed to think of today."[1]

Malcolm's family had not given up on him, despite his rebellious ways. His first visitor at Charlestown was Ella Collins who later recalled what it was like seeing her younger brother behind bars: "It was not a very pleasant visit. Malcolm was as jive-talking, cocky, and unrepentant as ever. He showed no remorse or concern about family anxiety and seemed to believe that his only problem was being caught, that the next time he would be a smarter hustler. When I left . . . I was as upset as I had ever been with him."[2]

The same type of hustling Malcolm participated in on the streets also took place in prison, only with subtle differences. For example, Malcolm arranged bets for other prisoners, and he used ingredients from the kitchen to mix a crude cocktail that would get him high.

Over time, Malcolm calmed down, mostly thanks to his meeting a fellow inmate named John Elton Bembry. Bembry, better known by the nickname of Bimbi, was a well-respected, older black inmate. Not surprisingly, he and Malcolm met when Malcolm purposely bumped into him in the prison yard, looking to start something. Despite the way they met, the two men eventually became friends, and the well-read Bimbi encouraged

Malcolm to use his noticeable intelligence and read some books. Educate yourself, Bimbi told him. Malcolm resisted at first but then gave in. Soon, he was reading everything he could find in the prison library. He also began to educate himself in other ways, such as by taking correspondence classes in English and Latin. To learn new words, Malcolm would copy them out of the dictionary onto a piece of paper. He was obsessive about doing so.

Reading opened Malcolm's mind and showed him there were other ways of thinking far different from what he believed or had even been taught. Books helped him become more educated and expand his vocabulary. He could not get enough of them. The hours of reading under the dim lights of his prison cell weakened his eyesight and caused Malcolm to need glasses. He got a pair of horn-rimmed ones, and the studious look they gave him became one of his defining characteristics for years to come.

In January 1947, Malcolm was transferred to another Massachusetts prison, the Concord Reformatory. Prisoners were transferred for various reasons, and it was a common practice to do so. Malcolm even used his newfound love for reading and learning to help himself receive one such transfer. When he learned a prison in Norfolk, Massachusetts, had an experimental program that focused on helping reform prisoners and offered them more freedoms than both Charleston and Concord, Malcolm—with the help of his sister—applied for admission. In February 1948, he was accepted into the program and transferred to the Norfolk Prison Colony. The facility there was state of the art, as far as prisons go, and had many good amenities, including a large library.

Despite his stubbornness, various members of Malcolm's family continued to write him letters. One such letter from his brother Reginald helped change Malcolm's life forever. In the letter he sent to Malcolm, Reginald told his brother to stop eating pork and smoking cigarettes. It was important that he keep his body pure. This would help get him out of prison.

Reading opened Malcolm's mind and showed him there were other ways of thinking different from what he believed or had even been taught.

Malcolm did not understand how these seemingly random things would lead to his release, but he followed his brother's instructions. When Reginald later came for a visit, Malcolm began to understand why his brother was telling him to make these odd changes in his life. Reginald, and several other members of Malcolm's family, had joined a religious movement called the Nation of Islam.

Founded in Detroit, Michigan, in 1930, the Nation of Islam was modeled after Islam, an ancient religion that began in the Middle East. The millions of people across the world who follow Islam are called Muslims. Muslims believe God—or Allah, as they call him— revealed all his knowledge to a prophet named Muhammad, who then began preaching the word of the Koran, the holy book of the Muslims. Nation of Islam followers were called Black Muslims.

When Malcolm was introduced to the Nation of Islam, the movement's leader was a small black man named Elijah Muhammad. Muhammad, born on October 7, 1897, in Sandersville, Georgia, was the son of former slaves. His birth name was Elijah Poole, and he changed his last name to Muhammad after he joined the Nation of Islam in 1931. He became leader in 1934, and the number of Black Muslims in the United States grew significantly under his control. Nation of Islam mosques sprung up across the country.

The principle beliefs of the Nation of Islam immediately appealed to Malcolm. As one author put it, the black nationalist religious group placed a "strong emphasis on black pride, history, culture, and unity . . . [and an] unblinking assertion that white men were devils, a belief that led Muhammad and his followers to advocate black separation from white society."[3]

It was easy to imagine Malcolm falling for a religion with such beliefs, which he promptly did. At the core, the Nation of Islam's beliefs were similar to the message preached some two decades earlier by Marcus Garvey and his many followers—including Malcolm's father—that blacks needed to live separately from whites. Muhammad believed blacks were members of the powerful "original" race and were getting along well together until they had been enslaved by whites. Many blacks in the United States who believed they were being oppressed by the white man believed in the message of the Nation of Islam and became followers of Elijah Muhammad.

Reginald used straight talk to sell his brother on the Nation of Islam. It was a language to which Malcolm could easily relate. Reginald said:

> You don't even know who you are. . . . [T]he white devil has hidden it from you, that you are of a race of people of ancient civilizations, and riches in gold and kings. You don't even know your true family name, you wouldn't recognize your true language if you heard it. . . . You have been a victim of the evil of the devil white man ever since he murdered and raped and stole you from your native land in the seeds of your forefathers.[4]

Malcolm came around to believing what Reginald had told him. Now twenty-three years old, Malcolm finally had his purpose in life. The teachings of the Nation of Islam and Elijah Muhammad spoke to him. He did believe that he had lived his life at the mercy of the white man who, in his mind, had constantly tried to keep him down. He thought about when his teacher had told him he could not be a lawyer. He thought about how his family had been attacked by white supremacists. He thought about his father's death.

The principle beliefs of the Nation of Islam immediately appealed to Malcolm.

Malcolm spent every moment he could learning more about his new infatuation. He did this, of course, by reading as much as he could, whenever he could. He mostly read history. One author said Malcolm was particularly affected by "the library's extensive collection of books and pamphlets about the captive Africans who had been taken to America in rat-infested ships, sold into slavery, and chained and whipped like miscreant dogs."[5] Such stories did nothing to improve Malcolm's already-negative attitude toward white people.

After he felt he had educated himself enough on the subject not to be embarrassed doing so, Malcolm wrote a letter to Elijah Muhammad. Muhammad wrote back, telling Malcolm he was not the criminal and should not be in jail. The real criminals, Muhammad said, were the whites who had made him commit the crimes in the first place, because he had no other way to succeed in the white man's world. The letter also included some money for Malcolm.

It was 1949 by the time Malcolm began following Muhammad's teachings. That same year, Malcolm began preaching them to anyone who would listen. In addition to the pork and cigarettes he already had relinquished, he swore off alcohol and drugs of any kind. He also practiced his public speaking by debating anyone he could on any subject at any time.

On March 23, 1950, Malcolm was transferred back to Charlestown State Prison because he refused to receive a shot that would protect him against Concord's contaminated water. He was now back in the same filthy prison where he had started serving his sentence. He spread the word of the Nation of Islam to every black prisoner he could. He even took his cause to a Bible study class he said was being taught by "a tall, blond, blue-eyed (a perfect 'devil') Harvard Seminary student."[6] When the class finished its discussion of the apostle Paul, Malcolm struck. He said: "I stood up and asked, 'What color was Paul?' And I kept talking, with pauses, 'He had to be black . . . because he was a Hebrew . . . and the original Hebrews were black . . . weren't they?' He had started flushing red. You know the way white people do. He said 'Yes.' I wasn't through yet. 'What color was Jesus . . . he was Hebrew, too . . . wasn't he?'"[7]

After some thought, the instructor answered. He said, "Jesus was brown."[8] The scene he caused at the Bible study elevated Malcolm to legendary status at Charlestown, and everyone wanted to talk about what he had done. Malcolm used each chance he had to chat with others as an opportunity to talk about Muhammad and the Nation of Islam.

This time, his parole was granted, but certain conditions were placed on him.

In 1951, both Malcolm and his coconspirator, Shorty, went before the parole board, a group of people who have the power to let an inmate out of jail before he or she has served their entire sentence. The board makes its decision based on a number of factors. The board decided to parole Shorty but not Malcolm. Thus, Malcolm stayed at Charlestown, and Shorty returned to Boston. The next year, Malcolm again came before the parole board. This time, his parole was granted, but certain conditions were placed on him. The most important one was that he had to show that he had a job waiting for him when he got out of prison. Malcolm's older brother Wilfred helped with that. Wilfred worked at a furniture store in Detroit and convinced his boss to hire Malcolm when he was released. Malcolm did not seem to mind that the store where he would be working made its money by preying on the poor, oftentimes blacks, selling cheap furniture to customers for inflated prices, and offering credit to those who needed it.

Prior to his parole, Malcolm's family had decided that Detroit would be a much better place for him to be than Boston. His sister Ella Collins said it was "because the police there [in Boston] would use any excuse to constantly harass him. They knew him as an undisciplined, jive-talking, conk-haired, zoot-suit-wearing petty criminal and, we were sure wouldn't accept the fact that he had become a disciplined, self-respecting, focused black man who had diligently used his time in prison to vastly expand his knowledge of history and current affairs."9

Outside prison, Malcolm immediately began work on that new life.

Malcolm was released from prison on August 7, 1952. He was twenty-seven years old and had spent six and a half years behind bars. Immediately after he was released, he went to stay the night at Collins's house before leaving for Detroit the next day. When he arrived there, Malcolm was a changed man. He had used prison

as his personal seminary, or religious college, a place
to study and master the teachings of Elijah Muhammad.
One of Malcolm's friends said, "In prison, Malcolm
told us, he found his salvation, because in prison he
discovered Islam, which gave him a new life. Prison was
Malcolm's cocoon. Inside it, he reformed and educated
himself. Malcolm shed one life form so a new one could
be born."[10]

Outside prison, Malcolm immediately began work
on that new life. He joined the Nation of Islam's Temple
Number One in Detroit and began attending meetings
there. His devotion to the movement grew even stronger
on August 31, when he and other members of the
temple traveled to Chicago to see their leader speak in
person. Of all the people at the event, Elijah Muhammad
pointed to Malcolm and asked him to stand. Author
Bruce Perry wrote: "The Messenger explained to the
rest of the congregation that Malcolm had recently been
released from jail. He described how faithfully Malcolm
had corresponded with him from prison."[11] Muhammad
told his followers, "I believe that he is going to remain
faithful."[12] Muhammad soon drew Malcolm even closer
under his wing. Malcolm's own words make it easy
to understand why he became so faithful to Muhammad.
He said:

> [T]he religion of Islam had reached down into
> the mud to lift me up, to save me from being what
> I inevitably would have been: a dead criminal in
> a grave, or, if still alive, a flint-hard, bitter . . .
> convict in some penitentiary, or insane asylum.

> Or, at best, I would have been an old, fading
> Detroit Red, hustling, stealing enough for food
> and narcotics, and myself being stalked as prey by
> cruelly ambitious younger hustlers such as Detroit
> Red had been.[13]

At this time, Malcolm also made a huge symbolic
move to show his solidarity to the Nation of Islam and
his disdain for white men. Shortly after joining the
Detroit temple, Malcolm dropped his last name of
"Little" and replaced it with an "X." His reasons were
clear. He said:

> The Muslim's "X" symbolized the true African
> family name that he never could know. For me,
> my "X" replaced the white slavemaster name of
> 'Little' which some blue-eyed devil named Little
> had imposed upon my paternal forebears. The
> receipt of my "X" meant that forever in the nation
> of Islam, I would be known as Malcolm X. Mr.
> Muhammad taught that we would keep this "X"
> until God Himself returned and gave us a Holy
> Name from His own mouth.[14]

Some years later, when Malcolm made a pilgrimage
to Mecca, Saudi Arabia, the holiest city in Islam, he
would replace the "X" with the last name "Shabazz."

Malcolm remained more than faithful to the cause,
becoming one of its most-devoted followers. He fervently
recruited members to his own temple, which helped
him advance in power proportionally. By mid-1953,
Malcolm had become the assistant minister of the
Detroit temple. When Malcolm was off parole and thus
able to leave Detroit, his minister there sent him to

Boston to recruit members. Returning to the place where he had once been a criminal was a risky proposition for Malcolm. His sister and other family members had tried to keep him out of the city for fear the police there would only remember him as a criminal. But religion had changed Malcolm; he no longer worried about what the police would think because he knew he was not going to break any laws. He did talk with some of his old friends, but he avoided hanging out in the places he used to. He was now following the Nation of Islam's rules. Pool halls, alcohol, drugs, and even dancing were off limits.

Shortly after joining the Detroit temple, Malcolm dropped his last name of "Little" and replaced it with an "X."

Soon, Malcolm had recruited enough people to start a new temple in Boston. Appropriately, he became that temple's minister. It was the first of several head positions Malcolm would obtain over the next couple of years, as his tireless work for the Nation of Islam continued to be rewarded. His next leadership job came in Philadelphia in March 1954. Just two months later, Malcolm was named leader of Temple Number Seven in Harlem.

New York City's temple was only a storefront in a slum when Malcolm took over. But the potential for expansion in New York City was limitless. There were roughly 1 million blacks in the city, many of them dirt poor and open to any message that might convince them that change was possible. The Nation of Islam certainly offered that hope.

Malcolm's first step was to let the people know his temple existed. Just as he had in Detroit and Boston, Malcolm began promoting his temple. Malcolm was the salesman, and the Nation of Islam was his product. As had been the case in the other cities, his tactics worked, and membership of Malcolm's Harlem temple slowly grew. Membership numbers also grew in Detroit and Boston and other cities, such as Pittsburgh, Pennsylvania; Atlantic City, New Jersey; Cleveland, Ohio; and Miami, Florida. The Nation of Islam was becoming a strong player in the national religious scene, but a majority of people in the United States still had not heard of the organization. One high-profile event that happened in April 1957 changed all that.

The event began in Harlem, when a white police officer beat a drunken black man who was involved in a fight on the streets. A crowd gathered to watch the incident. In the crowd was a Nation of Islam member named Johnson Hinton, who shouted at the police to stop their beating. Hinton said a policeman then attacked him as he was leaving the scene.[15] The policeman said he accidentally bumped into Hinton.[16] Whatever the truth, what happened next is indisputable.

Hinton was arrested and taken to jail. Word of his plight quickly made its way back to members of Hinton's temple, who gathered outside the police station in protest. Soon, Temple Number Seven's leader got word and joined the protest. Malcolm went inside the jail and demanded to see Hinton. At first, he was told Hinton was not there and that no one knew where he was. Then, Malcolm was told Hinton was there but could not have visitors. By this point, thousands of blacks—temple members and others—had gathered outside. Malcolm told the police he would not tell the crowd to leave until he was allowed to see Hinton. Feeling the pressure of thousands of angry people outside, the police finally allowed Malcolm to see the prisoner.

When he saw Hinton, Malcolm said later, "[I]t was all I could do to contain myself. He was only semi-conscious. Blood had bathed his head, face, and shoulders. I hope I never again have to withstand seeing another case of sheer police brutality like that . . . I told the lieutenant in charge, 'That man belongs in the hospital.'"[17] Fearing a riot, the police obliged and called an ambulance that took Hinton to the hospital. Much of the crowd marched through the streets behind the ambulance, all the way to the hospital. Others who were not originally involved joined in along the way.

> **Malcolm was the salesman, and the Nation of Islam was his product.**

At the hospital, the marchers gathered outside to wait to hear about Hinton's condition. When Malcolm came out and assured everyone that Hinton was receiving excellent medical care, the crowd left. Even the police were impressed by the power Malcolm had over such a large crowd of strangers. They could not believe one man could have so much control. From that time on, police were assigned to every scheduled speech Malcolm made to help with crowd control. Oftentimes, those speeches would draw thousands of people. Malcolm's words were usually defiant and always antiwhite. The following is an excerpt of a speech he gave in Philadelphia, where he refers to the white man as "the devil":

> You hear us talking about the white man and you want to go away and tell him we have been subversive. Here is a man who had raped your mother and hung your father on his tree, is he subversive? Here is a man who robbed you of all knowledge of your nation and your religion and is he subversive? Here is a man who lied to you and tricked you about all things, is he subversive? . . . Black man [sic] all over the planet are subversive to this devil. . . . You's better listen or you will be taken off the planet along with the devil. This wicked government must be destroyed. . . . The devils have lost their power and the only thing they can do is try to frighten black men who are still dead.[18]

Malcolm did not advocate violence in and of itself; rather he advocated self-defense and self-protection—such as the right to bear arms—for himself, his family, and his fellow blacks.

Though it may sound as if Malcolm was recommending violence, he was not. Malcolm did not advocate violence in and of itself; rather he advocated self-defense and self-protection—such as the right to bear arms—for himself, his family, and his fellow blacks. He felt they had the right to retaliate against injustices levied against them, by any means necessary. Where applicable, that included violence.

The Hinton incident was one of several high-profile situations where blacks in the United States stood up and spoke out against what they believed to be racial discrimination. Similar stances were being taken across the United States during what was called the civil rights movement. In America, the movement proper lasted from about the mid-1950s into the early 1970s, though its roots can be traced back to the late 1800s and early 1900s to separatist Booker T. Washington and to W. E. B. DuBois, who championed integration. Among the best known of the individual civil rights stances occurred on December 1, 1955, in Montgomery, Alabama. The person making the stand was a woman named Rosa Parks.

After finishing a hard day of work as a seamstress at a department store, Parks hopped on Montgomery's Cleveland Avenue bus for her ride home. She took an empty seat in the fifth row, the first row of the "Colored Section," where blacks were allowed to sit. When a white male passenger came on board, Parks refused to give him her seat. At the time, it was customary for blacks to surrender their seats to whites. But Parks, who was a member of the National Association for the Advancement of Colored People (NAACP), would not. Parks was arrested for her defiance.

Rosa Parks in 1956, after she refused to give up her seat on a bus.

What happened next had a huge impact on the entire United States. In protest of Parks's arrest, blacks were asked to boycott the Montgomery bus line and to refuse to ride any bus until black and white riders alike were treated equally. Tens of thousands of notes were sent out to places blacks frequented. They said: "We are . . . asking every Negro to stay off the buses Monday in protest of the arrest and trial. . . . You can afford to stay out of school for one day. If you work, take a cab, or walk. But please, children and grown-ups, don't ride the bus at all on Monday. Please stay off the buses Monday."[19]

The planned one-day boycott soon turned into a week, then a month, then a year. Without any black passengers, the bus line lost a lot of money. The months of negative media coverage was a huge public relations nightmare for the bus line. Eventually, the protest worked. On December 21, 1956, Montgomery's bus line was officially desegregated. Riders of any color now were allowed to sit wherever they wanted on Montgomery's buses.

The organization that planned the boycott was called the Montgomery Improvement Association. Leading that group was a black Baptist minister named Martin Luther King Jr., who soon would become a nationally known leader of the civil rights movement. King's approach to evoking change involved using calm, peaceful, and loving tactics. He did not believe in using violence to promote his cause, but rather nonviolent civil disobedience.

King's beliefs differed vastly from Malcolm's angry and often-aggressive tactics.

Not that Malcolm could not be loving on occasion, especially to his fellow Black Muslims. And it often was hard for Malcolm to resist a woman who was both a Black Muslim and beautiful. It turns out such a woman did exist. Moreover, to Malcolm's surprise, she had been right under his nose for quite a while.

Chapter 5

Rising Through the Ranks

Sister Betty Sanders was a perfect potential partner for Malcolm. Tall, attractive, and dark-skinned, she also was a member of the Nation of Islam's Harlem Temple. When the two met, Betty already had shed her last name of Sanders and had, like Malcolm, adopted the letter X as her last name. She was studying to become a nurse. According to Malcolm's autobiography, her schooling was about to end, however, because her parents had discovered she was a Black Muslim and had threatened to cut her funding because of it. Malcolm wondered, "What would happen if I just *should* happen, sometime, to think about getting married to somebody? For instance Sister Betty X—although it could be any sister in any temple, but Sister Betty X, for instance, would just happen to be the right height for somebody my height, and also the right age."[1]

Elijah Muhammad had told Malcolm that tall men like Malcolm should not marry short women, because

Elijah Muhammad (far right) and Malcolm X (left) in 1961 in Chicago.

they did not look right together. He also said the perfect
age for a man's spouse should be half of his age plus
seven years. If that was true then Betty, who was
twenty-three, was perfect for the thirty-two-year-old
Malcolm. Despite these facts, Malcolm still had
reservations. He said, "I was so shocked at myself, when
I realized *what* I was thinking I quit going anywhere
near Sister Betty X, or anywhere I knew she would be.
If she came into our restaurant and I was there, I went
out somewhere. I was glad I knew that she had no idea
what I had been thinking about."[2]

Malcolm hesitated to ask Betty to marry him for a
couple of reasons. First, he had been rejected by several
women in the past, and he was afraid another woman
might tell him no. Malcolm did not want to deal with
that personal rejection. Second, Malcolm felt it was
necessary to gain approval from Elijah Muhammad
before marrying. So he arranged for his mentor to
meet Betty by flying her to Chicago to attend some
classes there. Muhammad met her and approved of her.
After all that, Malcolm decided to propose. Never the
romantic type, Malcolm approached the proposal as
if it were just another business deal he was conducting.
He called her on the phone and asked her if she
wanted to get married, and she agreed. The marriage
ceremony was conducted in much the same manner: as
straightforward and quickly as possible. It happened on
January 14, 1958, in Detroit. Malcolm later explained
the reason he was not very romantic. He thought acting
that way was fake and that it led to misconceptions

Malcolm X holds daughter, Ilyasah, while getting into a car in New York in 1964.

about what the marriage actually would be like on a day-to-day basis. He said:

> All of that Hollywood stuff! Like these women wanting men to pick them up and carry them across thresholds and some of them weigh more than you do. I don't know how many marriage breakups are caused by these movie- and television-addicted women expecting some bouquets and kissing and hugging and being swept out like Cinderella for dinner and dancing—then getting mad when a poor, scraggly husband comes in tired and sweaty from working like a dog all day, looking for some food.[3]

In November, Betty gave birth to the couple's first daughter, Attallah. She and Malcolm would have five more daughters together. Qubilah was born in 1960; Ilyasah, named after Elijah Muhammad ["Ilyasah" is the feminine form of "Elijah"] was born in 1962; and Gamilah was born in 1964. In 1965, twins Malaak and Malikah were born.

In November, Betty gave birth to the couple's first daughter, Attallah.

It is a safe bet Betty knew early on that being married to Malcolm would not be anything like a fairy tale. The couple's first house was one good indication of that. It was a humble two-bedroom place in Queens, New York. Malcolm had an office in the attic, and he would often spend large amounts of time in there reading, praying, and sometimes even sleeping. Malcolm did not even own the house: the Nation of Islam did and allowed Malcolm to use it. The house was one of the many gifts the Nation provided to its top promoter. Malcolm also received a small amount of pay each week, a car, and travel expenses. The life he and Betty lived was far from extravagant.

The Nation of Islam also owned Muhammad's home in the South Side of Chicago, but it was much nicer than Malcolm's was. Muhammad's home was an eighteen-room Victorian mansion, complete with armed guards outside. Muhammad and the Nation of Islam also operated several thriving businesses. They owned grocery stores, apartment buildings, and many other properties.

The house was one of the many gifts the Nation provided to its top promoter.

Malcolm did not look at the lifestyle discrepancies between himself and Muhammad as a problem. Malcolm was a very spiritual man and believed that his eternal life was far more important than whatever happened to him during the time he spent living on earth. He had no doubt the Nation of Islam would take care of him and his family, and that was all he desired. He still worked as hard as he could to spread the message of the Nation of Islam and Muhammad.

There are indications that Betty was not happy with the small amount of payment and possessions Malcolm was receiving for his tireless work. One of her peers said Betty "tried to explain to [Malcolm]—as we all did at one time or another—that you can't live off the crumbs. You makin' millions of dollars for this man. You don't own the house you live in. You don't own the car. You barely own the clothes on your back. But he loved Elijah so much he couldn't see the forest for the trees."[4]

Despite his wife's concerns, Malcolm still was willing to submit to the sacrifice. In many ways, Muhammad was like the father that Malcolm had barely known. He also was Malcolm's mentor, and Malcolm would do just about anything to keep him happy and successful. In 1959, that meant becoming the Nation of Islam's ambassador and traveling across the world to spread the group's message. Malcolm's charisma and excellent public speaking skills gained him large audiences everywhere he went. People in other countries wanted to know what this Black Muslim uprising in the United States was all about. Muhammad appointed Malcolm to be the one to tell them.

In addition to his using live speaking engagements to further his cause, Malcolm also began using the media. He began writing a weekly column for the Los Angeles *Herald-Dispatch* newspaper. His columns, like his speeches, were full of antiwhite, pro-black Muslim propaganda:

> Our idea of "heaven," after being brainwashed by the white man's Negro puppets, (Negro preachers), seemed to revolve around INTEGRATION (Gen. 6:2) and uniting (not with OUR OWN KIND but) with the wicked race of white Christians who had kidnapped, robbed and enslaved us. We really "loved OUR ENEMIES!" No people had ever been treated as badly or as cruelly as the white race treated us, YET WE LOVED THEM. . . . We

Malcolm X holds a copy of *Muhammad Speaks* in 1963.

"forgave those who despitefully used us" . . .
we literally "turned the other cheek." . . . [We]
actually began to worship the artificial beauty of
the slave-masters' pale, leperous-looking white
woman. . . . [A]nd at the same time we were
treating our own beautiful Black women as if
THEY were mere animals.[5]

When considered in context with the history of
slavery, Malcolm's comments seem a lot less harsh.
Black slaves from Africa were indeed treated poorly
by whites and "kidnapped, robbed and enslaved," as
Malcolm said they were. During what was called the
Middle Passage portion of the slave
ships' voyage to the United States,
Africans were beaten, chained, and
tortured. The conditions the black
men, women, and children were placed
under were so deplorable that many
died of disease and starvation—and
some took their own lives—long before
they reached American shores. Even
after the Emancipation Proclamation of
1863 freed slaves, and the Thirteenth
Amendment to the Constitution in 1865 made slavery
illegal in the United States, blacks still were not treated
equally.

The power of the press was vital, Malcolm realized, to further spread the Nation of Islam's message.

Malcolm's articles caused quite a stir in both black
and white communities. The power of the press was
vital, Malcolm realized, to further spread the Nation of
Islam's message. So, in 1961, Malcolm helped found

the Nation's own newspaper. It was called *Muhammad Speaks*, and was, of course, named after the prophet Elijah Muhammad. Nation of Islam members sold the newspaper on street corners across the country. It soon became a powerful publication, and each issue was read by tens of thousands of people. The proceeds from its sales went to fund Nation of Islam causes, such as building new temples and improving the ones that already existed. Each issue, readers were treated to a column from Muhammad, called "Mr. Muhammad Speaks," and stories filled with pro-Nation propaganda. There were stories about separatist Marcus Garvey, whom Malcolm's father had followed three decades earlier. Malcolm also wrote for the newspaper. His basic message, as always, was black independence. In one article, titled "Muslim Minister Rips 'Token' Integration," Malcolm wrote:

> Our people have been here in America for over 400 years. We have been so-called "free" for 100 years . . . Why then are the masses of our "people" still jobless and homeless? Why are we still the last hired and the first fired? . . . [T]he Honorable Elijah Muhammad is asking that some separate territory (not a state, but several states) be set aside for the 20 million ex-slaves, and with the help of ALLAH he will show us how to solve our problems. We won't be forcing ourselves into white communities, schools and factories. WE WILL SET UP OUR OWN! AND RUN OUR OWN![6]

Television also helped spread the Nation of Islam's message. One TV show in particular played an enormous role in introducing the Nation to mainstream America. Called *The Hate That Hate Produced,* the show aired in July 1959. It was narrated by journalist Mike Wallace, who went on to become a legend in the broadcasting industry. The program was an in-depth look at the rise of the Nation of Islam, and it talked about the message of black supremacy that the Nation was trying to spread. It featured interviews with Muhammad and Malcolm X and showed scenes from well-attended Nation of Islam rallies across the United States. The program's title referred to the Nation of Islam's alleged "hate" for white people and the belief that it was a product of the hate that white people had for blacks.

Television also helped spread the Nation of Islam's message.

The airing of the documentary on mainstream television had a huge impact on the country. Many white people became afraid of the movement. Author Bruce Perry explained in his biography of Malcolm exactly what he thought white people found most alarming: "One reason was Malcolm's acknowledgment that Elijah Muhammad taught that the serpent in the Garden of Eden was not a snake, but a symbol for the white man. The aspect that really frightened white viewers was the footage about the University of Islam— the elementary school the Nation ran in Chicago—where black pupils were taught, from kindergarten on, that whites were devils."[7] It was the truth, but many were not even aware it was going on.

The TV show led to coverage of the Nation by other mainstream media outlets. Books were written about Black Muslims. Malcolm said people were constantly calling. Malcolm's sister Ella Collins said her brother told her many of those phone calls were negative and full of hate. She also said that the head of the Ku Klux Klan, a man named J. B. Stoner, even wrote a letter to a New York City police officer commenting on the show. The letter said:

> I have received a report from one of our Klansmen on the New York police force informing me that the nigger Muslims are in rebellion against White law and order. . . . [I am] an expert on black Muslims and have kept up with their infidelic activities for many years. . . . I assure you that they are much more dangerous to White Christian rule in New York than you realize. You and I must join forces to stop the black Muslims now or they will soon drive every White person out of New York City. The largest city in the world will then be an all nigger city of black supremacy.[8]

Stoner then offered the unnamed police officer the help of his Klansmen: "I think 5,000 Klansmen could clean up Harlem for you if you would give them police badges and N.Y. police uniforms to wear instead of their Klan uniforms. They will leave their robes at home so New York niggers won't know that your police reinforcements are White Christian Klansmen."[9] Stoner's words may seem harsh and highly bigoted, but a large segment of America's population at the time still felt exactly the same way he did about blacks.

The show helped Malcolm become a well-known public figure across the United States. Malcolm basked in the spotlight his newly elevated status afforded him. He took pleasure in fielding questions from reporters and debating those whose opinions differed from his. Elijah Muhammad still was the leader of the Nation of Islam, but Malcolm had become its best-known spokesperson. This began to create tension between the two men that later would lead to significant problems.

The Nation of Islam's increased exposure introduced its teachings to more people, but with the growth came more negative scrutiny. The Federal Bureau of Investigation (FBI), which had opened a case file on Malcolm shortly after his release from prison and also had an open file on Martin Luther King Jr., took an even bigger interest in Malcolm's activities. The agency even hired members of the Nation of Islam to spy on him. What Malcolm did in September 1960 made the FBI pay even closer attention to what he was doing. That was the month Cuban leader Fidel Castro came to the United States to talk at the United Nations (UN) in New York City.

The show helped Malcolm become a well-known public figure across the United States.

The United States was not on the best of terms with Cuba when Castro came to visit. Just one year earlier, the United States government had stood behind Castro as he led the charge to overthrow the dictatorship of Fulgencio Batista. However, after Castro came into

Fidel Castro (left) speaks with Malcolm X.

power, some U.S. leaders began to believe Castro was trying to turn his country into a Communist nation, similar to the Soviet Union. It was a path the United States did not want him to follow. In March 1960, President Dwight D. Eisenhower called for economic sanctions against Cuba, and he directed the Central Intelligence Agency (CIA) to begin planning the overthrow of Castro's regime.

On September 26, Castro gave a speech denouncing the policies of the United States. Though his speech was an astounding four and a half hours long, one does not have to read the whole thing to understand his tone. A small excerpt will do:

> Notes from the U.S. State Department began to rain down on Cuba. They never asked us about our problems, not even to express sympathy or because of their responsibility in creating the problems. They never asked us how many died of starvation in our country, how many were suffering from tuberculosis, how many were unemployed. No. Did they ever express solidarity regarding our needs? Never. Every conversation we had with the representatives of the U.S. government centered around the telephone company, the electricity company, and the problem of the land owned by U.S. companies. The question they asked was how we were going to pay. Naturally, the first thing they should have asked was not "How?" but "With what?"[10]

Castro's speech was the final straw for the United States. The United States severed all ties with Cuba in January 1961, and invaded the country in April.

Malcolm had very little contact with Castro during his visit to the United States. He met with the Cuban leader for just thirty minutes, at the celebrated Hotel Theresa in Harlem, where Castro had decided to stay after his delegation had been treated poorly at the more upscale Shelbourne Hotel in midtown Manhattan.

However, those thirty minutes were enough for the FBI to take note of the visit and to place it into Malcolm's ever-growing file. The report said:

> [D]uring his visit he [Malcolm] told CASTRO, in reference to CASTRO himself, that usually when one sees a man whom the United States is against, there is something good in that man. To this, CASTRO replied that only the people in power in the United States are against him, not the masses. [Malcolm] further expressed the opinion that any man who represented such a small country that would stand up and challenge a country as large as the United States must be sincere.[11]

By all accounts, Malcolm knew the FBI was monitoring him almost from the time the agency began doing so. That did not stop him from doing the same things he had been doing. Malcolm continued promoting the Nation of Islam, debating all comers, granting interviews, verbally attacking his enemies, and giving speeches across the country. In fact, sometimes he would even toy with the FBI. He once said:

> One of those blue-eyed things [a white person] had the nerve, a couple of years ago, to go to Philadelphia and tell the Muslims, "They say Brother Malcolm is . . . in New York livin' with a

white woman." Imagine that! I told the brothers, "Next time the old F.B.I. come and tell you that, you tell him that if I'm in New York livin' with a white woman, it's his mother. . . . And since she's livin' with me as he says, I can tell him what his mother is *like*. What she *does*! How *nasty* she is!"[12]

The mother insults were part of a black tradition called "playing the dozens," where instead of fighting with violence, people would battle verbally, often attacking family members of their opponent. Today, playing the dozens is most commonly known as telling "your mama" jokes.

Malcolm's rise to prominence in the Nation of Islam also helped his family members. His brother Wilfred became head of the Nation's Detroit temple, and Philbert became head of a few smaller temples in Michigan.

Soon, Malcolm himself began having his own problems with the leadership of Elijah Muhammad.

Meanwhile, Muhammad's health began to become an issue. It had been declining for some time, and he and his sons were starting to think about who would be the Nation's next leader. Malcolm had long been the Nation's number-two man, and, in 1962, had been awarded the title of national minister. Some in the Nation believed Malcolm already was, in everything but name, their leader.

Soon, Malcolm himself began having his own problems with the leadership of Elijah Muhammad. One of them happened when Nation of Islam member Ronald Stokes was shot and killed by police on April 27, 1962, in Los Angeles. When that happened, it was Malcolm who flew to Los Angeles the next day to help keep the black public calm during the aftermath.

It was a dangerous and tricky political situation. Stokes was the secretary of the Los Angeles temple and worked at a dry cleaning business. On the day of the incident, suspicious police confronted Stokes and another worker as they were unloading clothes from a car. First, an argument, then a fight, broke out. A crowd gathered, more police arrived, and shots were fired. In the end, eight men had been shot: one police officer and seven Black Muslims. Stokes died at the scene. The patrol officer who shot him testified that Stokes had been unarmed but had "raised his hands in a menacing way."[13]

> **So all Malcolm could do was hope for justice through the legal system.**

The *Los Angeles Times* said the incident had been a riot by the Black Muslims, but it was never proven that any of them even had guns.[14] If that was true, Malcolm wondered, why was it necessary for police to use theirs? Outraged over the incident, Malcolm said:

> I'm telling you they came out of those cars—and we have enough witnesses to hang them—with their guns smoking. Chief Parker knows this, Mayor Yorty knows this and every police official in the city knows that. They didn't fire no warning

shots in the air. They fired warning shots point-
blank at innocent, unarmed defenseless Negroes.
As I say two of the brothers were shot in the back.
. . . It is the police who should be on trial here in
Los Angeles.[15]

Malcolm believed so strongly in the innocence of his
fellow Muslims because he knew what Stokes, and every
other Muslim, had been trained to do if approached by
police. Malcolm said the training told them that they
should do the following:

[I]mmediately submit to their questioning. If they
say, "Come on, let's go to the station house," we
go, voluntarily. And you can read in police files
across the country that in their own reports, they
admit this. The only time there is ever any violence
involving Muslims with policemen is when the
policemen attack the Muslims. [Those] who were
shot down in front of the mosque, in front of the
temple, in front of the house of worship, they were
shot down in cold blood.[16]

A photographer who was on the scene described
what he saw. He said, "I arrived at the mosque in Los
Angeles after the shooting took place, and there was
great sadness amongst the people, you know. Malcolm
was walking back and forth, shaking his head saying,
'They're going to pay for it, they're going to pay for
it, they're going to pay for it, they're going to pay
for it.'"[17] But Muhammad had told him not to commit
any violence. So all Malcolm could do was hope for
justice through the legal system. He did not get it.
The officer who shot and killed Stokes was acquitted

by a jury, and fourteen Black Muslims were tried for assault. Eleven of them were convicted and sent to prison.[18]

Malcolm did claim to have gained some revenge a little more than a month after the Stokes incident. That revenge came on June 3, when a group of Atlanta's upper-crust white citizens was flying back from a month-long tour of Europe, and their plane crashed shortly after taking off from Paris. The crash killed 130 people, and the people of Atlanta were devastated by the massive loss of life. However, Malcolm saw the crash as payback for what had happened to Stokes. He told a crowd in Los Angeles, "I would like to announce a very beautiful thing that has happened. I got a wire from God today. He really answered our prayers over in France. He dropped an airplane out of the sky with over 120 white people on it because the Muslims believe in an eye for an eye and a tooth for a tooth. We will continue to pray and we hope that every day another plane falls out of the sky."[19] Malcolm never apologized for his statement but later said he probably would not make the same statement again if he were in a similar situation.

Malcolm also came to question Elijah Muhammad's morals. Was he following every rule he was telling others to follow? Was he practicing what he was preaching? Malcolm soon discovered the answers were "no" to both those questions. One of the main covenants of the

> **Malcolm also came to question Elijah Muhammad's morals.**

Nation of Islam was being faithful to your spouse. But when longtime rumors that the married Muhammad had slept with many of his secretaries—and even had fathered some illegitimate children—started to surface, Malcolm began to have more doubts about the man he had spent the past several years faithfully devoted to. The two men had had philosophical differences before. But when they did, Malcolm always had followed what his leader wanted him to do. But these accusations of infidelity, which Malcolm knew to be true, were too much for him to handle. Several members of the Nation of Islam had left their respective temples because of it. Malcolm knew he had to talk to Muhammad about the situation. In April 1963, Malcolm flew to Phoenix, Arizona, to confront his mentor in person.

Muhammad recently had left his impressive home in Chicago for one of similar grandiosity in Phoenix, where the desert air would be more favorable to his chronic asthma. When Malcolm began to question Muhammad about his extramarital affairs, the prophet tried to defend himself by talking about events in the Bible where adultery had been committed. Muhammad said he was only doing the same thing those in the Bible had, so it was fine for him to do so. He made no mention of the Koran, which frowns upon adultery. Muhammad's attempt at justification did not convince Malcolm. It only helped sever Malcolm's ties with the man he had fought so hard to promote and to defend. Malcolm returned to New York, trying to sort out what he had heard and to figure out what, if anything, he was going to—or even could—do about it.

Malcolm later spoke out on how disappointed he was at what Muhammad had done:

> Well, he represented himself to us as a prophet who had been visited by God. . . . I actually thought that he had been taught and commissioned by God to solve the problems of our people in America. Then I came into the knowledge of something in his own personal life that he admitted to me when I confronted him with it. But when it came to him taking the steps that a man would take to correct the mistake, I found that his own ability to be a man was lacking. When I ceased to respect him as a man, I could see that he also was not divine. There was no God with him at all.[20]

Chapter 6

A Bitter Split

More than a quarter of a million people gathered around the Lincoln Memorial in Washington, D.C., on August 28, 1963. They came to the nation's capital from across the country and from all walks of life. They were blacks and whites; doctors, lawyers, and common folk; rich and poor. Several celebrities were there, too, including singers Joan Baez and Bob Dylan and actors Marlon Brando, Paul Newman, and Sidney Poitier. It was a festive and historic occasion.

Everyone in attendance shared one common goal. They were there to participate in the March on Washington for the Jobs and Freedom civil rights event. The event was scheduled to let the U.S. government know its people wanted legislation passed that would ensure every American was treated equally, regardless of race.

Martin Luther King Jr.—the same minister who had organized the blacks' boycott of buses in Montgomery,

Alabama, after the Rosa Parks incident—delivered one of the most famous speeches in history on that day in Washington, D.C. It became known as his "I Have a Dream" speech. It spoke of King's vision for America and his hope for a day when everyone would be treated equally, regardless of the color of his or her skin. The speech ended with a powerful message:

> And when this happens, when we allow freedom to ring, when we let it ring from every village and every hamlet, from every state and every city, we will be able to speed up that day when all of God's children, black men and white men, Jews and Gentiles, Protestants and Catholics, will be able to join hands and sing in the words of the old Negro spiritual, "Free at last, free at last. Thank God Almighty, we are free at last."[1]

Most people considered the march a rousing success. But Malcolm X was not like most people. Although he, like King, was among the most prominent civil rights leaders in America and stood to benefit from the gathering, Malcolm did not support it. He called it the "Farce on Washington" and said it could not really be successful because it was too peaceful and there were too many white people there. He said the whites "engulfed it. They became so much a part of it [that] it lost its original flavor. It ceased to be angry. It ceased to be impatient. In fact, it ceased to be a march. It became a picnic."[2]

He told another journalist, "They went down, they sang some songs, they marched around. They went and marched between the feet of the two dead presidents,

Malcolm X speaks in Harlem in 1963.

Lincoln, and, what's his name, Washington. They carried signs, they shouted. When they left Washington the civil rights bill hadn't passed yet. . . . So everything has passed except that which is supposed to help Negroes."[3]

Malcolm never had been a fan of King's, whose philosophy of blacks and whites living together in harmony greatly differed from Malcolm's philosophy of separating the races. Malcolm once explained how he disagreed with King:

> The goal of Dr. Martin Luther King is to give Negroes a chance to sit in a segregated restaurant beside the same white man who had brutalized them for 400 years. The goal of Dr. Martin Luther King is to get Negroes to forgive the people who have brutalized them for 400 years by lulling them to sleep and making them forget what those whites have done to them. But the masses of black people in America today don't go for what Martin Luther King is putting down.[4]

Though their tactics may have differed, each man had his large legion of followers. But when Malcolm criticized the harmonious March on Washington, many blacks began to wonder what Malcolm's motives really were. After an event that occurred that fall, they would question them even more.

When President John F. Kennedy was assassinated in November 1963, in Dallas, Texas, Elijah Muhammad ordered Malcolm and all other members of the Nation of Islam not to comment on the president's death. Kennedy was a very popular president, even among blacks, and the entire country was saddened by his death. However,

Martin Luther King Jr. (left) and Malcolm X in 1964.

Malcolm did not follow his leader's orders. When asked what he thought about Kennedy's assassination, he told one reporter that the president's killing was a case of "the chickens coming home to roost,"[5] meaning that Kennedy was somehow responsible for his own death. Malcolm added, smiling, "Chickens coming home to roost never did make me sad; they've always made me glad."[6] Malcolm later elaborated on his comments and said they were taken out of context. He said, "I said the hate in white men had not stopped with the killing of defenseless black people, but that hate, allowed to spread unchecked, finally had struck down this country's Chief of State."[7]

> **Clay was a Black Muslim and had known Malcolm for a couple of years.**

Muhammad did not see any humor in Malcolm's comments, which ran the following day in newspapers all across the country. He summoned Malcolm to Chicago to meet with him and suspended Malcolm from the Nation of Islam for a period of time, which Malcolm often said would be ninety days. Publicly, Malcolm appeared to be fine with Muhammad's decision, even saying at time that he felt he deserved it. But deep down, the suspension angered Malcolm and signaled the beginning of the end of his involvement with Muhammad and the Nation of Islam. Malcolm later said that his words were taken out of context and that Muhammad had been looking for something to suspend him for.

To take his mind off his situation and to get out of

New York—where members of his own temple had begun speaking out against him and where he was not allowed to speak—Malcolm headed to Miami, Florida. A young boxer named Cassius Clay was there training for a big fight against heavyweight champion Sonny Liston and had invited Malcolm to come watch him train and to help him mentally prepare for the fight. Clay was a Black Muslim and had known Malcolm for a couple of years.

Malcolm was ringside on February 25, the day of the fight. The bigger and older Liston was heavily favored to beat Clay, but, prior to the fight, Malcolm gave Clay a pep talk. He said: "This fight is the *truth*. . . . It's a modern Crusades—a Christian and a Muslim facing each other with television to beam it off Telstar for the whole world to see what happens! . . . Do you think Allah has brought about all this intending for you to leave the ring as anything but the champion?"[8]

When the fight began, the twenty-two-year-old challenger did not back down from the champion. By the end of the fight's sixth round, Liston was the one who was hurting. When the seventh round was set to begin, Liston could not continue. The outspoken Clay had defied the odds to become the heavyweight champion of the world. The day after the fight, Clay announced to the world that he was a Muslim, which he had been for a while, and that he had changed his name to Muhammad Ali.

The time he spent with Ali may have provided a much-needed break for Malcolm, but all it did was delay

Malcolm X (left) and Muhammad Ali in 1964.

Muhammad Ali

Muhammad Ali was well on his way to becoming a legendary American long before he knocked out Sonny Liston in February 1964 to become the boxing's world heavyweight champion. Born Cassius Marcellus Clay Jr. on January 17, 1942, in Louisville, Kentucky, Ali began boxing at the age of 12 after his bike was stolen and he told a police officer he wanted to beat up whoever had taken it. By chance, the policeman also was a boxing trainer and offered to teach the sport to the youngster. Ali proved a talented student and eventually won the gold medal in the light-heavyweight division in the 1960 Olympics. He turned professional shortly thereafter. Controversies followed Ali throughout his professional career. The biggest one came in 1967, when Ali—a recently converted Black Muslim—refused to serve in the U.S. military during the Vietnam War on the grounds that his religion forbade him to fight. The move angered many people, and also the federal government, which found Ali guilty of refusing induction into the military. He eventually cleared his name on appeal but was stripped of his boxing title and banned from the sport for three-and-a-half years. Ali returned to the ring in 1970 and fought many other memorable bouts, including the "Fight of the Century" against Joe Frazier in 1971 and the "Rumble in the Jungle" against George Foreman in 1974. Ali regained his world title during that latter fight. Ali retired from boxing in 1981, announced he had Parkinson's disease a few years later, and began devoting his life to philanthropy.

what seemed to be an inevitable outcome: Malcolm was going to break away from the Nation of Islam. In March, he did just that. Malcolm held a press conference announcing that he was resigning from the Nation of Islam. He said he believed it was time for him to start a movement of his own. He named his new Islamic organization Muslim Mosque, Inc. It was to be a religious and political organization. Malcolm said:

> [W]e are still Muslims—we still worship in a mosque and we're incorporated as a religious body. . . . The Muslim Mosque, Inc. will have as its religious base the religion of Islam which will be designed to propagate the moral reformation necessary to up the level of the so-called Negro community by eliminating the vices and other evils that destroy the moral fiber of the community. . . . But the political philosophy of the Muslim Mosque will be black nationalism, the economic philosophy will be black nationalism, and the social philosophy will be black nationalism.[9]

The split with the Nation of Islam also destroyed Malcolm's relationship with boxer Muhammad Ali, although Malcolm would not readily admit that his good friend had broken off their friendship. Malcolm said on the record that he did not believe Ali had made any negative statements about him, even though Ali did several times.

Malcolm said members of his Muslim Mosque could also continue being members of the Nation of Islam if they wanted to. But that was before he began hearing rumors that the Nation of Islam was plotting to have him killed.

On March 26, Malcolm met Martin Luther King Jr. for the first and last time. Though the two civil rights leaders had been known to disagree with the other's methodology, the meeting appeared to be a cordial one. King had just finished debating civil rights legislation in Washington, D.C., when Malcolm met him in a hallway. The two men shook hands, and most of the photos taken of the meeting show both men wearing wide smiles across their faces.

Malcolm was going to break away from the Nation of Islam.

When Malcolm split with the Nation of Islam, he had to forfeit all the possessions the Nation owned. That included his house, his car, and the income the group was paying him. Malcolm did not give up the house he and his family were living in without a fight, which he took to court and eventually lost. Before he did, however, Malcolm's refusal to turn the home over to the Nation of Islam angered its members. One member said: "That house . . . is ours, and the nigger don't want to give it up. Well, all you have to do is [to] go out there and clap on the walls until the walls come tumbling down, and then cut the nigger's tongue out and put it in an envelope and send it to me. And I'll stamp it 'APPROVED' and give it to the Messenger."[10]

Malcolm's departure from the Nation of Islam left him nearly broke, and it placed a severe damper on the next plan he hoped to execute. However, with financial help from his sister, Malcolm was able to make his desired pilgrimage to Mecca, Saudi Arabia. The trip, called a hajj, is mandatory for all adult Muslims who can afford it and are healthy enough to make it. Mecca is considered the center of the Muslim religion. It is the birthplace of the Prophet Muhammad and of Islam, the religion he started thirteen hundred years prior to Malcolm's trip.

For more than a month, Malcolm toured the Middle East and Africa. He was fascinated with what he saw. Mecca was full of Muslims of all skin colors, not just blacks. In Mecca, all the Muslims were treated equally. Everyone was united for the same purposes: to worship and respect their god, Allah, and to practice peace and unity. During his time there, Malcolm sent a postcard home to author Alex Haley, who had been interviewing Malcolm and helping him write his autobiography. The postcard said Malcolm had "eaten from the same plate with fellow Muslims whose eyes were bluer than blue, whose hair was blond, blonder than blond, whose skin was whiter than white. . . . And we were all the same."[11]

For more than a month, Malcolm toured the Middle East and Africa.

Malcolm told another friend that Mecca had changed his narrow-minded way of thinking. He said:

> I have some explaining to do. . . . I had very little formal education, eight grades. I am self-educated. . . . [C]onsequently, I believed everything the

Honorable Elijah Muhammad told us, and the
Honorable Elijah Muhammad told us that Islam
was a black man's religion—exclusively—and that
the blue-eyed devils could not get close to Mecca,
that they would be killed if they tried to enter that
sacred city. In Mecca I saw blue-eyed blonds
worshipping Allah just as I was, kneeling right
beside me, so obviously the Honorable Elijah
Muhammad had lied.[12]

Despite all the years he had spent preaching it,
Malcolm's trip to Mecca made him realize all white
men were not devils, after all. His voyage changed his
thinking on many issues. Malcolm learned that the
traditional religion of Islam was different from what
Muhammad had taught him. Malcolm returned to
America a changed man, although he still did not believe
blacks and whites should integrate. Malcolm also had
a different name. The man who had been born Malcolm
Little, then had become Malcolm X, had changed his
name again, this time to the traditional Muslim name of
Hajj Malik El-Shabazz. Most people, however, continued
to refer to him as Malcolm X, and Malcolm appeared to
be fine with that.

His trip to Mecca was a successful venture for
Malcolm, but his recently founded Muslim Mosque
was not. He had a hard time recruiting members. He did
not abandon the organization, but he did decide to start
another one. He called this one the Organization of Afro-
American Unity (OAAU). The OAAU called on blacks
to control all their own institutions, and it promised to
help them do so. The first OAAU meeting was held June

28, 1964, in New York. The speech Malcolm gave on
that day became one of his most famous of all time.
He said, in part:

> We don't care how rough it is. We don't care how
> tough it is. We don't care how backward it may
> sound. In essence it only means we want one
> thing. We declare our right on this earth to be
> a man, to be a human being, to be respected as a
> human being, to be given the rights of a human
> being in this society, on this earth, in this day,
> which we intend to bring into existence by any
> means necessary.[13]

Malcolm's departure from the Nation of Islam—and
the many negative things he had said about its leader,
Elijah Muhammad—had left him with many enemies.
The newspaper he said he helped found, *Muhammad
Speaks*, began running negative articles about him. The
paper once reported: "Only those who wish to be led to
hell, or to their doom, will follow Malcolm. The die is
set, and Malcolm shall not escape."[14] Malcolm believed
this to be true and interpreted it to mean that his split
with Islam probably would end with his own violent
death. In another article in *Muhammad Speaks*, a Black
Muslim minister named John Shabazz wrote: "But YOU,
Malcolm, were treated like a SON by The Messenger. . . .
[H]e did more for you than your real parents ever could,
or were inclined to do, even if they could. If it were
not for the Messenger, you would still be just another
unheard-of penny-ante Harlem hustler. The Bible
accurately describes you as 'a dog returning to his own
vomit.'"[15]

Hajj

The hajj is the trip to Mecca, Saudi Arabi, which every Muslim capable of doing so is required to make at least once in his or her lifetime. The hajj begins in the twelfth month of the Islamic calendar, which is based on a lunar cycle instead of the solar cycle used in the United States. This means the hajj sometimes occurs in the summer and sometimes in the winter. To prepare for the hajj, the person must first enter a pure spiritual state free of arguing and sexual relations called ihram. Other aspects of the hajj include the wearing of special plain clothes that help make everyone attending equal in terms of class and culture and the performing of many rituals, including circling the Ka'bah, or small shrine, seven times while praying. Pilgrims also travel seven times between the hills of Safa and Marwa. The hajj lasts roughly five days and its end is marked by a large celebration called the Eid al-Adha. The hajj is the fifth of the Five Pillars of Islam. The others include the profession of faith, daily prayers, giving to charity, and fasting during the month of Ramadan.

Muslims must face the Ka'bah, the black shrine in the center of the Great Mosque in Mecca, when they pray.

Many people grew to hate Malcolm, and he began receiving many death threats. Black Muslims constantly drove by his house. Malcolm's wife, Betty, said the people driving by were vicious. Even though Malcolm no longer believed that his followers should carry weapons, he bought a gun for his house, taught Betty how to use it, and told her to shoot anyone who tried to come through their door. Malcolm often was forced to contact police, and sometimes he was granted police protection. Federal Bureau of Investigation (FBI) files from the time show that Malcolm was indeed being harassed. One report said: "Malcolm X was contacted on July 5, 1964, [and advised] that orders to kill him, MALCOLM, have come from Chicago."[16] Another report stated that an anonymous phone caller said Malcolm was going to be killed. Malcolm even talked about those threats on the radio. The FBI said that on a June 13, 1964, radio program in Boston, "MALCOLM stated that several threats had been made on his life during the last five months. Malcolm then remarked that recently on a radio program in Chicago known as 'Hot Line,' JOHN ALI, National Secretary of the Muslims, had been asked by a telephone caller if it was true that the Muslim Movement was trying to kill MALCOLM X. According to MALCOLM, JOHN ALI replied that they were trying to kill MALCOLM X and that he should be killed."[17]

> **Many people grew to hate Malcolm, and he began receiving many death threats.**

The threats of harm, which regularly occurred even when Malcolm was conducting interviews, did not deter him from his mission of promoting the OAAU. He encouraged blacks to take part in the political process and to become active in their communities. He gave speeches, appeared on talk-radio programs, and was interviewed by dozens of magazines and newspapers. He even traveled to Africa to meet with the leaders of several countries to try to gain their support for what he was trying to accomplish. He wanted to put pressure on the United Nations to reprimand the United States for its treatment of blacks.

The irony was that because Malcolm spent such a long time in Africa, the OAAU and the nearly defunct Muslim Mosque suffered from lack of leadership. Malcolm tried to spin his absence as being a positive thing for the organization. When he was in Africa, Malcolm sent a letter to his followers back home in the United States. It read: "I've stayed away this summer and given all those who want to show what they can do the opportunity to do so. . . . I'm going to be away for at least another month. During that time you can . . . make the Muslim Mosque and OAAU a success, or you can destroy both organizations. It's up to you."[18] Despite his words, not many blacks were willing to follow the "new" Malcolm. He tried to spin that fact, as well.

Sixty of his followers greeted Malcolm at the airport when he returned to the United States on November 24, 1964. He picked up right where he had left off, speaking in public, sitting down for interviews, and doing everything in his power to promote his mission of black equality. In February 1965, Malcolm and Martin Luther King Jr. took their respective civil rights battles to Selma, Alabama. At the time, blacks in the South still were struggling with certain civil rights, including the ability to vote in some elections. A campaign for black voting rights was being held in Selma. King already was in jail when Malcolm arrived in town, having been arrested during a protest on February 2. King recently had won the Nobel Peace Prize, and he was more popular than ever, with every move he made being reported on by the press. It would be logical to think that Malcolm would be happy that a fellow black man had been given one of the most prestigious honors given to a person and had used that honor to help spread his message of equality for blacks. But Malcolm was not happy. He said: "I don't think that King got the prize because *he* had solved our people's problem, cause *we* still got the problem. He got the Peace Prize, and *we* got the problem. And so I don't think he should have gotten the medal for that. . . . I don't want the white man giving me medals. If I'm following a general, and he's leading me into battle, and the enemy begins to give him awards, I get suspicious of him."[19]

An organization called the Student Nonviolent Coordinating Committee—which later distanced itself from its nonviolent stance by changing its name to the Student National Coordinating Committee—had invited Malcolm to Selma. Many of those in the audience feared his rebellious words might start a riot. But they did not. In fact, his speech talked about how blacks needed to come together for the common good. He told the media in Selma he believed any effort to give black people the right to vote was a good thing, even if it came from King.

The next day, Malcolm hopped a plane to London, where he spoke at the First Congress of the Council of African Organizations. Then he left for Paris, where he was to speak to the Federation of African Students. When Malcolm's plane landed there, French authorities took him into custody and would not let him enter the country. No official reason was given, but author Bruce Perry said the officials "hinted that the U.S. State Department had asked them to bar him from France."[20]

In fact, his speech talked about how blacks needed to come together for the common good.

A news story on the incident ran in the *Times* (London). It read: "Malcolm X, the American Negro militant leader, was refused entry to France this morning and ordered to return to London. The decision to refuse him entry was taken on the grounds that his presence could disturb public order."[21] Malcolm was quoted in the article as saying, "The authorities would not even let me contact the American Embassy. I was shocked. I thought I was in South Africa. I did not even get as far as immigration control. They took me to a room where I was kept in seclusion by three policemen.

I might as well have been locked up. They would not let me speak to anyone or telephone."[22]

Whatever the reason, Malcolm was placed on the next plane to London, where he spoke two days later at the London School of Economics. On February 13, Malcolm flew back to New York.

Before he left for Europe, Malcolm had talked in detail with writer Alex Haley about how he knew that some bad and very angry people were out to get him, and what he thought about that. He said, "I am only facing the facts when I know that any moment of any day, or any night, could bring me death. This is particularly true since the last trip I made abroad. I have seen the nature of things that are happening, and I have heard things from sources which are reliable."[23]

Malcolm may have believed something dreadful would eventually happen to him, but he had no idea when. As it turns out, that misfortune was waiting for him when he got home.

Chapter 7

A Violent Death

Although a judge had ordered them to vacate their New York home by January 31, 1965, Malcolm and his family still were living in it when he returned from Europe in mid-February. The Nation of Islam, which owned the home, was not happy with that fact and had asked the police to do something about it. A judge was set to hear the case on February 15. No one knew the house would not be the same when he did.

Malcolm was asleep when the destruction hit. It was shortly after 2:30 A.M. on February 14, after all, and he had just returned from a long, stressful trip overseas. His wife and four children were asleep, too, as were most people in New York at that time of morning. Nevertheless, all six people in the household awoke abruptly at almost the exact same time, after Malcolm heard the sound of broken glass. Shortly after, he noticed his living room was on fire. Someone had tossed a firebomb through a window and into his home. He and

Betty gathered their children and rushed them outside. Malcolm then went back inside the brick house to retrieve some personal belongings. His wife, who was pregnant at the time of the fire, later talked about how she was impressed with her husband's courage in the face of danger. Betty said, "I always knew he was strong, but at that hour I realized how great his strength was."[1]

Malcolm, Betty, and their four young girls stood outside in the cold winter night and watched as their house burned. It was the second time in his life Malcolm had stood by and watched as flames destroyed the place he called home. The first time, he was a young child in Michigan. This time, he was a man.

Though no one was ever charged with the crime, Malcolm believed he knew who was to blame for the firebombing and let the media know it the next day. He claimed his house "was bombed by the Black Muslim movement on the orders of Elijah Muhammad. . . . I have no compassion or mercy or forgiveness for anyone who attacks sleeping babies. . . . The only thing I regret is that two black groups have to fight and kill each other off. Elijah Muhammad could stop the whole thing tomorrow just by raising his hand. Really, he could. He could stop the whole thing by raising his hand, but he won't. He doesn't love black people."[2]

For its part, the Nation of Islam denied any wrong-doing. In fact, one of its leaders, Joseph X, said he believed Malcolm himself had started the fire "to get publicity."[3] He told one newspaper, "We own the place.

In 1965, Malcolm X's house was firebombed.

He was going to be evicted. Why would we bomb our own property?"[4]

Although it may sound ridiculous that Malcolm would set fire to his own home—especially with his wife and children inside—it is not that far-fetched of a theory. Malcolm was about to lose the house anyway, so what did he have to lose by setting the fire, as long as he knew for sure he could get his family out before they were harmed? At least then, the Nation of Islam could not have it, either. Malcolm strongly denied he played any role in the fire. He said, "If anybody can find where I bombed my own house they can put a bullet through my head."[5] Just as they had in 1929 when young Malcolm's house had burned to the ground, questions surrounded the cause of this blaze. Many never were officially answered. Days later, at 9 A.M. on February 18, the family was officially evicted from the home, for the last time, and Malcolm moved the last of his salvaged belongings out four hours later.

After the fire, Malcolm's wife and children went to stay at a nearby friend's house. Malcolm did not go with them. He spent the next few hours preparing to catch a plane to Detroit, where he was scheduled to speak. When he arrived at his hotel in Detroit, Malcolm was visibly shaken from what had happened to him and his family. He was given a sedative by a doctor to help calm him down. He then slept until it was almost time for him to deliver his speech.

It is easy to understand why Malcolm would appear shaken. In addition to the fire, the threats against

Malcolm's life had intensified in recent weeks. In one incident, described by Alex Haley, the ghostwriter of Malcolm's autobiography, Malcolm was involved in a car chase in Los Angeles that could have turned deadly. The story goes:

> [Malcolm] was in a car with others and they came to some kind of tunnel. [That's when] they saw another car behind them, in which they knew were people who were enemies: They were all members of the Nation of Islam, but they were all anti-him. And as this other car drew closer—it seemed, like, in this tunnel—he had a cane; he, Malcolm, had a walking cane—and he slipped that cane out the back window and worked it behind so that it looked like a rifle barrel. And the other car fell back rapidly, and they got away without difficulty.[6]

> **Malcolm continued to tell anyone who would listen how he believed he was a marked man.**

Now, with the fire at his home, even his family appeared to be at risk. Malcolm continued to tell anyone who would listen how he believed he was a marked man. He said he expected to be killed, but the unsettling thing was that he never knew when it was going to come.

Malcolm stood true to his word and continued to work. On February 15, he was back in New York, speaking to a crowd of six hundred people at the Audubon Ballroom at a rally for his Organization for Afro-American Unity. According to the FBI, Malcolm talked about the firebombs that had hit his home and accused the Nation of Islam of doing it. Then, he "claimed that a conspiracy exists between the NOI [Nation of Islam] and the Ku Klux Klan that is not in the best interest of the black people. He alleged that the NOI and the Klan have agreed to leave each other alone and that the Klan has offered land in North Carolina to the NOI for the latter's 'separate state' for Negroes plan."[7]

For the time being, Malcolm decided to remain separated from his family, and he checked into a hotel. He did it to protect his family from whoever might be coming after him. He and Betty did go looking for a house of their own, however. They even agreed to put the home in someone else's name to help keep their lives anonymous. Author Russell J. Rickford said that Malcolm was trying to save his relationship with his wife by spending more time with her. His frequent traveling had put a strain on his marriage. Rickford wrote: "Malcolm had begun clearing his calendar of appearances and had made an appointment . . . for the next week to draw up a will. . . . He was finally slowing down long enough to handle domestic matters. His relationship with Betty had nearly dissolved. Perhaps it now had a fighting chance. . . . He said he understood what he had put her through.

> **Malcolm's next speech was scheduled for February 21, back at the Audubon Ballroom in Harlem.**

He apologized for the hardship and vowed that change was coming."[8]

But before he could fully clear his calendar, Malcolm had some more big speeches to get through. His next one was February 18, at Columbia University in New York. There, he gave a speech titled, "The Black Revolution and Its Effect Upon the Negroes of the Western Hemisphere."

Malcolm's next speech was scheduled for February 21, back at the Audubon Ballroom in Harlem, where he had talked just six days earlier at an OAAU rally. The day before the February 21 speech, Malcolm called Haley to tell him he had some doubts as to whether it was indeed the Nation of Islam that was after him, as he had been saying all along. Malcolm said:

> [Y]ou know, I'm going to tell you something, brother—the more I keep thinking about this thing, the things that have been happening lately, I'm not all that sure it's the Muslims. I know what they can do, and what they can't, and they can't do some of the stuff recently going on. Now, I'm going to tell you, the more I keep thinking about what happened to me in France, I think I'm going to quit saying it's the Muslims.[9]

He did not say who he thought might be harassing him.

On the morning of February 21, Malcolm called his wife from his hotel room, and he asked her if she would get the children dressed and bring them to the Audubon Ballroom to hear him speak that afternoon. She agreed to do so, although she was surprised he had asked; he had told her earlier that she should stay home because he did not think it would be safe for her to attend.

Most of the ballroom's four hundred seats were filled by the time Betty and her four daughters arrived at the venue, but they found a few open seats in the front row. Most of the people there were members of Malcolm's Organization for Afro-American Unity, there to hear another inspirational message from their charismatic leader. Malcolm's friend introduced him by saying, "I present to you . . . one who is willing to put himself on the line for you . . . a man who would give his life for you."[10]

Malcolm smiled at the introduction and began to speak. He said, *As-salaam alaikum*. Peace be with you. The crowd responded back: *Wa-alaikum salaam*. And peace be with you. Malcolm then noticed a commotion a few rows back in the audience. Malcolm heard it, looked out into the crowd, and said, "Let's cool it, brothers."[11] Those would be his last words. A shotgun blast ripped through the wooden podium Malcolm was standing behind, hitting him in the chest and knocking him backward over two empty chairs. Malcolm fell to the ground. The shotgun fired again. Someone then tossed a smoke bomb inside the ballroom, likely to create a diversion. Two black men then jumped from their seats, pulled out their pistols, and began firing them into Malcolm's prone body.

Malcolm fell to the ground.

One of Malcolm's bodyguards shot one of the gunmen in the leg as he tried to flee. The man kept

The Audubon Ballroom after the shooting of Malcom X.

going, making it outside, where he was beaten by the crowd that had followed him out. Police had to stop the people from killing the gunman. The man turned out to be a twenty-two-year-old black man named Talmadge Hayer. Eyewitness reports from the scene said there were possibly four or five total assassins, but they all safely escaped.

Inside the ballroom, Malcolm's pregnant wife had thrown her daughters to the floor during the commotion and shielded them with her body. When the shooting began, she screamed, "They're killing my husband!"[12] Onstage, a few people gathered around Malcolm, who was bloodied and motionless. One woman who said she was a registered nurse said, "I rushed to the stage even while the firing was going on. I don't know how I got on the stage, but I threw myself down on who I thought was Malcolm—but it wasn't. I was willing to die for the man. I would have taken the bullets myself. Then I saw Malcolm, and the firing had stopped, and I tried to give him artificial respiration. I think he was dead then."[13] An undercover police officer named Gene Roberts also tried to give Malcolm artificial respiration.

Meanwhile, several of Malcolm's supporters rushed across the street to a hospital, took a stretcher, and brought it back for Malcolm. He was wheeled out of the venue and taken to the hospital. A famous photograph taken at the time shows Malcolm lying on a stretcher, being escorted by several police officers.

But it was too late. Their thirty-nine-year-old black leader—admitted to the hospital under the name "John

Malcolm X is carried out on a stretcher after being shot at the Audubon Ballroom.

Doe" because no one had yet officially identified him—was dead on arrival. An autopsy showed that Malcolm died of pellets from a shotgun and bullets from two different pistols, a .45 caliber and a 9 mm.

That he might die at such a young age did not surprise Malcolm. He had known it might be coming. He even had said so:

> To speculate about dying doesn't disturb me as it might some people. I never have felt that I would live to become an old man. Even before I was a Muslim—when I was a hustler in the ghetto jungle, and then a criminal in prison, it always stayed on my mind that I would die a violent death. In fact, it runs in my family. . . . [I]f I take the kind of things in which I believe, then add to that the kind of temperament that I have, plus the one hundred percent dedication I have to whatever I believe in—these are ingredients which make it just about impossible for me to die of old age.[14]

He also told another person, just a few weeks before he died:

> You'll find very few people who feel like I feel that live long enough to get old. . . . [A] black man should give his life to be free, but he should also be willing to take the life of those who want to take his. It's reciprocal. And when you really think like that, you don't live long. And if freedom doesn't come to your lifetime, it'll come to your children. Another thing about being an old man, that never has come across my mind. I can't even see myself old.[15]

News of Malcolm's death spread quickly. The front

page of the next day's *New York Times* ran a photo of Malcolm being wheeled to the hospital on a stretcher, underneath the headline "Malcolm X Shot to Death at Rally Here."[16] The article quoted one police officer as saying, "[T]his is a result, it would seem, of a long-standing feud between the followers of Elijah Muhammad and the people who broke away from him, headed by Malcolm X."[17] Muhammad, as could be expected, denied any connection to the murder. The *Times* article quoted Malcolm's lawyer as saying, "Malcolm X died broke, without even an insurance policy. Every penny that he received from books, magazine articles and so on was assigned to the Black Muslims before he broke with them, and after that to the Muslim Mosque, Inc."[18]

> **"Malcolm X Shot to Death at Rally Here."**

Police and civil rights leaders feared Malcolm's death might start an all-out war between his followers and the followers of Elijah Muhammad. That never transpired, although there were some isolated incidents. For example, the day after Malcolm was killed, a firebomb was thrown through a fourth-floor window at the Nation of Islam's Temple Seven, the Harlem mosque where Malcolm had once been leader. Six firefighters were hurt battling the blaze, which destroyed the building. Police had been standing guard outside, but no one was seen committing the crime. Bomb threats also were called in across the city of New York. One Harlem newspaper ran an editorial on its front page hoping to help stop a riot from occurring. It read: "None of these . . . emotions can be, or should be used, as an excuse to set off disorder and rioting such as took place in our community a few months ago. Despite what has been said about him, Malcolm X had a great respect for law and order and no one can truthfully say that he ever precipitated a riot. . . . Let's give Malcolm the warmth and respect that is due him. But let's be cool about it."[19]

After he heard the news, Martin Luther King Jr. asked his followers not to resort to violence. So did the leader of the NAACP. King also sent a telegram to Malcolm's widow, telling her he was sorry for her husband's death. The telegram said that he respected what Malcolm was trying to accomplish for the black race, even if he did not agree with his methodology.

> **That Malcolm had touched an enormous number of lives became apparent shortly after his death.**

That Malcolm had touched an enormous number of lives became apparent shortly after his death. Tens of thousands of mourners poured into the Unity Funeral Home in Harlem to view Malcolm's open casket. The line into the funeral home extended for blocks. Viewing had to be stopped several times while police searched for bombs.

Many Harlem shops were shuttered for a period in tribute to Malcolm. Many stores also closed for Malcolm's funeral service, which was held Saturday,

Malcolm's wife, Betty, at his graveside in 1965.

February 27, at the Faith Temple Church of God. As could be expected, security at the church was tight, with hundreds of uniformed police officers on hand. The church was filled to capacity, and thousands of people who could not get in stood by outside. Actor Ossie Davis, and his wife, actress Ruby Dee, performed the eulogy for their friend Malcolm. Davis called Malcolm "our own black shining Prince!—who didn't hesitate to die, because he loved us so."[20] After the service, Malcolm was taken to Ferncliff Cemetery outside New York City in Hartsdale, where he was buried under the name Hajj Malik El-Shabazz, the name he had taken after his trip to Mecca. Several other well-known people are also interred at Ferncliff, including actresses Joan Crawford and Judy Garland and entertainer Ed Sullivan.

> **By the time their investigation was complete, police had arrested three members of the Nation of Islam.**

By the time their investigation was complete, police had arrested three members of the Nation of Islam, charging each one with the murder of Malcolm X. It took police ten days to capture three suspects. The police settled on just three suspects even though eyewitnesses had said there were up to five assassins. Investigators also thought there likely were more people involved. But in the end, the men charged with Malcolm's murder were Hayer, who had been arrested at the scene; Norman 3X Butler; and

Thomas 15X Johnson. Their trial began on January 12, 1966, in New York City.

The prosecution had a strong case against Hayer. After all, he was the one who had been seen fleeing the scene of the crime, shot by a bodyguard, then mauled by the crowd until police arrived to arrest him. When they did so, they found a bullet that matched the murder weapon in his pocket. But the case against the other two defendants was not nearly as strong. There was no physical evidence against them, as there had been for Hayer. The only real evidence against Butler and Johnson was eyewitness testimony, and even that proved to be shaky at best.

Six weeks into the trial, after long claiming his innocence, Hayer took the stand and told everyone he had shot Malcolm. He added that his codefendants were innocent of the crime. Hayer said, "I just want the truth to be known that Butler and Johnson didn't have anything to do with this crime. I was there, I know what happened, I know the people that did take part in it, and they [Butler and Johnson] wasn't any of the people that had anything to do with it."[21] Hayer said someone had hired him to kill Malcolm, but he would not say who that someone was.

The jury was not swayed by Hayer's sudden change of opinion. After deliberating for more than twenty hours, the jury reached a verdict for all three of the defendants. The three men were found guilty of first-degree murder and faced mandatory sentences of life in prison, although they each would be eligible for parole in roughly twenty-seven years. Three men were in prison for Malcolm's murder, but there still were many unanswered questions about what had happened inside the Audubon Ballroom on February 21, 1965. Those unanswered questions would be the source of many debates for decades to come.

Chapter 8

"Sincere" Legacy

The Autobiography of Malcolm X was published a few months after Malcolm's death. The book, written by Malcolm through ghostwriter Alex Haley, was a smash hit. Millions of copies were sold to people looking for more insight into the man they had heard so much about. Although some historians believe many of the events Malcolm described in the book were exaggerated to suit his agenda, *Autobiography* still became required reading in classrooms across the country. The underlying theme of the book was black people's struggle for civil rights. Malcolm, of course, was one of the main leaders of that battle, which continued to be fought after his death.

Perhaps the best-known civil rights leader ever, and one of Malcolm's chief rivals, Martin Luther King Jr., suffered a fate similar to Malcolm's. On April 4, 1968, King was in Memphis, Tennessee, to lead a protest march for that city's striking black garbage workers.

Standing on the balcony of his hotel room in the early evening hours, King was shot in the neck. He died a short time later at the hospital. The death of King—who always had preached against violent acts—was followed by riots in several cities. A white convict named James Earl Ray was convicted of King's murder and sentenced to ninety-nine years in prison, where he died in 1998 at the age of seventy.

Over the years, other people who fought for civil rights also died tragically. One, white presidential candidate Robert Kennedy, younger brother of assassinated president John F. Kennedy, was shot and killed in June 1968, just two months after King's murder. Shortly after Malcolm's death, a group called the Black Panther Party was formed. The Black Panthers were a political organization that promoted a radical, pro-black agenda.

Many of its members—and many police officers and innocent bystanders—were killed in violent acts attributed to the Black Panthers.

In November 1965, Betty Shabazz gave birth to twin girls, Malaak and Malikah. After Malcolm's death, the grieving widow received thousands of cards, letters, and phone calls, a majority of them offering her condolences and telling her how great a man her husband was. Thanks to the donations and fund-raising efforts of Malcolm's friends and supporters, Betty and her daughters were able to purchase a large house in Mount Vernon, New York. Over the years, Malcolm's widow often lectured at colleges across the country and spoke at gatherings for certain organizations. Oftentimes, her pro-black messages sounded just like her deceased husband's. She told one crowd, "Unless there is peace for blacks there's going to be no peace for anybody else."[1] She also spoke out for women's rights.

The Nation of Islam continued trekking along under the leadership of Elijah Muhammad, until his death in 1975 at the age of seventy-seven. That is when Muhammad's son, Wallace, took over the organization, renamed it, and made several changes. The changes angered some members of the Nation and caused many of them to leave the group. One of those departing members, Louis Farrakhan, took the Nation of Islam name for his new group, which followed many of the same guidelines as Muhammad's group had.

Betty began saying she believed Farrakhan played a role in her husband's death.

The charismatic Farrakhan soon became the focus of the attention of Malcolm's widow. Betty began saying she believed Farrakhan played a role in her husband's death. In 1994, her second daughter, thirty-four-year-old Qubilah, was arrested for conspiring to murder Farrakhan, whom she believed played a main role in her father's killing. Qubilah made a deal with prosecutors, who allowed her to avoid going to trial if she sought psychiatric counseling, and she agreed to drug and alcohol treatment. In an unexpected move, Farrakhan issued a public statement saying he forgave Qubilah. A few months later, Betty met Farrakhan on stage at Harlem's Apollo Theater, where the widow and the man she had accused of playing a role in the death of husband shook hands in a show of peace.

The family trouble did not end with Qubilah's arrest. In June 1997, Qubilah's twelve-year-old son, named Malcolm after the grandfather he never knew, set fire to his grandmother's apartment in Yonkers, New York. Betty Shabazz suffered burns on more than 80 percent of her body during the fire. She died three weeks later at the age of sixty-one. She is buried next to her husband at Ferncliff Cemetery in Hartsdale, New York. Thousands of people visit the modest burial site each year.

Talmadge Hayer said he was recruited to kill Malcolm by two members of the Nation of Islam.

Shortly after the death of Elijah Muhammad, one of the men convicted of killing Malcolm changed the confession he had made at the trial, and he offered another version of what had happened to Malcolm. Talmadge Hayer said he was recruited to kill Malcolm by two members of the Nation of Islam because the Nation felt Malcolm had betrayed them. Hayer wrote at the time: "I thought it was very bad for anyone to go against the teaching of the Hon. Elijah, then known as the last Messenger of God. I was told that Muslims should more or less be willing to fight against hypocrites and I agreed [with] that. There was no money payed [sic] to me for my part in this."[2] Hayer went on to say that his codefendants,

Betty Shabazz

Following the death of her husband, Betty Shabazz made many of her own contributions to the American civil rights movement. At first she struggled to cope with Malcolm's assassination, but her resolve was soon strengthened by her own spiritual pilgrimage to Mecca. After the visit, she continued to raise her six daughters alone while simultaneously managing to earn a doctorate from the University of Massachusetts in 1975. She then went to work at Medgar Evans College in Brooklyn, New York. A private person by nature, Shabazz felt she had a duty as wife of one of the best-known black men of all time and helped carry on her husband's legacy and his work whenever she could. She played a key role in the renaming of one of the City Colleges of Chicago to Malcolm X College and worked tirelessly to maintain control over the use of her husband's name, while using it herself when necessary in her ongoing work to help underprivileged children. Her work was not overlooked. Following her untimely death in 1997, many American leaders released statements paying tribute to Shabazz, including then-President Bill Clinton and the Reverend Jesse Jackson. More than two thousand people attended her memorial service, including poet Maya Angelou and the governor of New York, George Pataki. Today, several tributes stand as testaments to her life's work, including the Malcolm X and Dr. Betty Shabazz Memorial and Educational Center, and the Dr. Betty Shabazz Health Center, both in New York, and the Betty Shabazz International Charter School in Chicago, Illinois.

Norman 3X Butler and Thomas 15X Johnson, had nothing to do with the crime.

Hayer's revised story had little effect on his or anyone else's situation, and all three men remained behind bars. They all changed their names to Muslim names, and eventually they were paroled from prison. In another strange irony, Butler became head of the Nation of Islam's Temple Seven after his release. The person he was found guilty of killing had transformed the same temple from a storefront in the ghetto into the Nation of Islam's most powerful branch.

There are also numerous streets and schools named after Malcolm.

Today, all across the United States, there are countless memorials and monuments commemorating the life of Malcolm X. The site of his childhood home in Omaha, Nebraska, is now listed on the National Register of Historic Places. The house Malcolm lived in there has since been torn down, but the property is owned and maintained by a nonprofit group called the Malcolm X Memorial Foundation. Located just off Malcolm X Avenue, the property has a large sign that reads "Malcolm X Birth Site" and another that tells his life story and ends with the words, "His teaching lives on." A similar sign exists in Lansing, Michigan. In cities across the country, there are also numerous streets and schools named after Malcolm. Even the site of his death has become a shrine of sorts. The Audubon Ballroom in Harlem is now home to the Malcolm X and Dr. Betty Shabazz Memorial and

Denzel Washington as Malcolm X in the 1992 movie, *Malcolm X*.

Educational Center. Highlights of the center include rare photos, videos, documents, and more.

In 1992, a major motion picture, simply titled *Malcolm X,* was released. The film, directed by Spike Lee, was a box-office smash. Actor Denzel Washington portrayed Malcolm, and actress Angela Bassett played the role of his wife, Betty. Washington won several awards for his portrayal of Malcolm, and he was nominated for a highly coveted Best Actor Academy Award. The plot of the film drew heavily from *The Autobiography of Malcolm X.*

The exact details of Malcolm X's death likely will never be known. Did orders for his death come from Elijah Muhammad, Louis Farrakhan, or another of the higher-ups in the Nation of Islam? Most historians agree that the Black Muslims were in some way responsible for Malcolm's death, but what role did people play in the 1965 shooting at the Audubon Ballroom in Harlem?

Throughout much of his adult life, Malcolm had talked about how he believed he would not live long enough to see old age, but he rarely mentioned what he hoped his legacy might be. Six weeks before he was murdered, he finally discussed that very subject. A newspaper reporter named Claude Lewis prompted the discussion, asking Malcolm how he would like to be remembered. Malcolm quickly answered:

> Sincere. In whatever I did or do, even if I make mistakes, they were made in sincerity. If I'm wrong, I'm wrong in sincerity. I think that the best a person can be—he can be *wrong*, but if he's

Followers of the Nation of Islam applaud a speech by their leader Louis Farrakhan during a convention in Detroit in 2007.

"In whatever I did or do, even if I make mistakes, they were made in sincerity."

sincere you can put up with him. But you can't put up with a person who's *right*, if he's insincere. . . . The times that we live in can rightfully be labeled, the Era of Hypocrisy. When white folks pretend that they want Negroes to be free, and Negroes pretend to white folks that they really believe that white folks want them to be free.[3]

Malcolm X was not an actor, but he played many roles during the thirty-nine years he was alive. He was the son of an outspoken black man, and he was a petty criminal jailed for his crimes. He was a loyal husband, a loving father, and a spiritual leader empowered with an eloquent speaking ability that could captivate an audience. In each of these roles, he achieved the goal he told Lewis he wanted to achieve. In each of these roles, Malcolm X was indeed sincere.

Chronology

1925—Malcolm Little is born on May 19 to Earl and Louise Little.

1929—The Little family home in Lansing, Michigan, burns to the ground.

1931—Malcolm begins kindergarten; Earl Little dies.

1939—Louise Little is declared legally insane and is committed to Kalamazoo State Mental Hospital in Michigan; Malcolm is sent to a juvenile detention home.

1941—Malcolm moves to Boston, Massachusetts, to live with his half sister Ella; he works various jobs, including on the railroad.

1942—He moves back to Michigan for a short period of time and then returns to Boston.

1943—He moves to Harlem, New York; he gains the nickname "Detroit Red"; he is found "mentally disqualified" for military service.

1946—Malcolm is arrested attempting to pick up a stolen watch he had left at a jewelry store; he is sentenced to eight to ten years in prison.

1949—He converts to the Nation of Islam religion; he begins to follow the teachings of Elijah Muhammad.

1952—He is paroled from prison at the age of twenty-seven; he gets a job at a Detroit furniture store.

1953—Malcolm becomes the assistant minister of the Nation of Islam temple in Detroit; he changes his name from Malcolm Little to Malcolm X; he founds and becomes minister of the first Nation of Islam temple in Boston.

1954—He becomes the acting minister of the Philadelphia, Pennsylvania, temple; he becomes minister of the New York temple.

1955—He becomes the minister of Philadelphia temple; Rosa Parks makes a stand on the bus in Montgomery, Alabama.

1957—Malcolm becomes the minister of the Detroit temple.

1958—He marries fellow Black Muslim Betty X; their daughter Attallah is born.

1959—Malcolm appears in the television documentary *The Hate That Hate Produced*; he travels to the Middle East and Africa as the National of Islam's ambassador.

1960—He meets with Cuban leader Fidel Castro in Harlem, New York; daughter Qubilah is born.

1961—He helps found the Nation of Islam newspaper *Muhammad Speaks*.

1962—He becomes the Nation of Islam's national minister; daughter Ilyasah is born; he flies to Los

Angeles, California, to calm the crowd after the death of Nation of Islam member Ronald Stokes.

1963—The March on Washington, D.C., takes place; Malcolm ignites controversy and is suspended by the Nation of Islam over some comments made about the death of President John F. Kennedy.

1964—Malcolm leaves the Nation of Islam and forms his own group, Muslim Mosque Inc.; he travels to Mecca, Saudi Arabia; he changes name to Hajj Malik El-Shabazz.

1965—His family home in New York is firebombed; he is assassinated February 21; twins Malaak and Malikah are born; *The Autobiography of Malcolm X* is published.

Glossary

bigoted—Intolerant of any race, creed, or opinion that differs from one's own.

boycott—To abstain from using.

charisma—A particularly strong appeal or charm.

Communist—An adherent of Communism, a system of government in which a single political party controls goods and services.

deed—A usually sealed written document containing a contract.

deport—To expel from a country.

dictatorship—A type of government where one person is in complete control.

discrepancies—Differences or inconsistencies.

divisive—Creating a division between two things.

hypocrisy—Pretending to believe something when one truly believes the opposite.

illegitimate—Born to parents who were not married to each other.

integration—Combining or uniting two or more parts.

jurisdiction—The power to exercise authority over something or someone.

methodology—The way one works toward a goal; procedure.

militia—A group of citizens organized to fight for certain rights, but not part of the regular army.

mosque—A place of public worship used by Muslims.

nationalism—A strong feeling of devotion to one's own country.

persecution—Punishment or harassment of a group or individual based on race, religion, or political beliefs.

propaganda—Facts or ideas spread to help further one's own cause or to damage another's cause.

propagate—To spread among people.

prophecy—A prediction of the future.

regime—A mode of rule or management.

temperament—The emotional qualities and personality traits of a person.

Chapter Notes

Chapter 1: A Vivid Memory

1. Alex Haley and Malcolm X, *The Autobiography of Malcolm X* (New York: Ballantine Books, 1992), p. 3.
2. Ibid.
3. Ibid.
4. Bruce Perry, *Malcolm X: The Life of a Black Man Who Changed Black America* (Barrytown, N.Y.: Station Hill Press, Inc., 1991), p. 9.
5. Ibid., p. 10.
6. Kofi Natambu, *The Life and Work of Malcolm X* (Indianapolis, Ind.: Alpha Books, 2001), p. 4.
7. Haley and Malcolm X, p. 3.

Chapter 2: Tragic Beginnings

1. "Earl Little, W. M. Townsend, and Robert Finney, Officers, International Industrial Club of Milwaukee, to President Calvin Coolidge," June 8, 1927, reproduced on *MarcusGarvey.com,* 2006, <http://www.marcusgarvey.com/wmview.php?ArtID=334> (February 12, 2009).
2. Bruce Perry, *Malcolm X: The Life of a Black Man Who Changed Black America* (Barrytown, N.Y.: Station Hill Press, Inc., 1991), p. 3.
3. Ibid., p. 5.

4. Alex Haley and Malcolm X, *The Autobiography of Malcolm X* (New York: Ballantine Books, 1992), p. 1.

5. Perry, pp. 3–4.

6. Ibid., p. 10.

7. "Man Run Over By Street Car," reproduced on *BrotherMalcolm.net,* May 19, 1999, <http://www.brothermalcolm.net/family/eldeath.html> (January 12, 2009).

8. Haley and Malcolm X, p. 14.

9. Ibid., p. 21.

10. Rodnell P. Collins with A. Peter Bailey, *Seventh Child*: *A Family Memoir of Malcolm X* (Seacaucus, N.J.: Birch Lane Press, 1998), p. 210.

11. David Gallen, *Malcolm X: As They Knew Him* (New York: Carroll and Graf, 1992), p. 122.

12. Perry, p. 39.

13. Haley and Malcolm X, p. 387.

Chapter 3: An Informal Education

1. Rodnell P. Collins with A. Peter Bailey, *Seventh Child*: *A Family Memoir of Malcolm X* (Seacaucus, N.J.: Birch Lane Press, 1998), p. 209.

2. Ibid., p. 11.

3. Alex Haley and Malcolm X, *The Autobiography of Malcolm X* (New York: Ballantine Books, 1992), p. 34.

4. Collins with Bailey, p. 22.

5. Ibid., p. 41.

6. Ibid.

7. Haley and Malcolm X, p. 137.

8. David Gallen, *Malcolm X: As They Knew Him* (New York: Carroll and Graf, 1992), p. 121.

9. Ibid., pp. 121–122.

10. Haley and Malcolm X, p. 137.

11. Gallen, p. 123.

12. "The Harlem Riot 1943," *TheHistoryBox.com,* n.d., <http://www.thehistorybox.com/ny_city/ riots/SectionIII/riots_article7a.htm> (January 12, 2009).

13. Ibid.

14. Ibid.

15. Collins with Bailey, p. 45.

16. Ibid.

17. Haley and Malcolm X, p. 110.

18. Clayborne Carson, *Malcolm X: The FBI File* (New York: Carroll and Graf, 1991), p. 108.

19. Haley and Malcolm X, p. 153.

Chapter 4: Falling for the Nation of Islam

1. Alex Haley and Malcolm X, *The Autobiography of Malcolm X* (New York: Ballantine Books, 1992), p. 153.

2. Rodnell P. Collins with A. Peter Bailey, *Seventh Child: A Family Memoir of Malcolm X* (Seacaucus, N.J.: Birch Lane Press, 1998), p. 70.

3. Michael Eric Dyson, *Making Malcolm: The Myth and Meaning of Malcolm X* (New York: Oxford University Press, 1995), p. 6.

4. Haley and Malcolm X, p. 164.

5. Bruce Perry, *Malcolm X: The Life of a Black Man Who Changed Black America* (Barrytown, N.Y.: Station Hill Press, Inc., 1991), p. 118.

6. Haley and Malcolm X, p. 193.

7. Ibid.

8. Ibid., p. 194.

9. Collins with Bailey, p. 83.

10. Curtiss Paul DeYoung, *Living Faith: How Faith Inspires Social Justice* (Minneapolis, Minn.: Fortress Press, 2007), p. 70.

11. Perry, p. 144.

12. Ibid., pp. 144–145.

13. Haley and Malcolm X, p. 293.

14. Ibid., p. 203.

15. Perry, p. 164.

16. Ibid.

17. Haley and Malcolm X, p. 238.

18. "Malcolm X Little," January 31, 1956, reproduced on *Federal Bureau of Investigation,* n.d., <http://foia.fbi.gov/malcolmx/malcolmx2.pdf> (March 12, 2009).

19. Rita Dove, "Rosa Parks: Her Simple Act of Protest Galvanized America's Civil Rights Revolution, *Time*, June 14, 1999, <http://www.time.com/time/time100/heroes/profile/parks02.html> (March 10, 2009).

Chapter 5: Rising Through the Ranks

1. Alex Haley and Malcolm X, *The Autobiography of Malcolm X* (New York: Ballantine Books, 1992), p. 232.

2. Ibid., pp. 233–234.

3. Ibid., p 236.

4. Russell J. Rickford, *Betty Shabazz: A Remarkable Story of Survival and Faith Before and After Malcolm X* (Naperville, Ill.: Sourcebooks, Inc., 2003), p. 144.

5. "Transcript of Malcolm X Weekly Column in Los Angeles *Herald-Dispatch*," November 21, 1957, reproduced on *Malcolm X: The FBI Files,* April 2004, <http://www.wonderwheel.net/work/foia/1958/021758-043058/articles/112157lahd.pdf> (March 12, 2009).

6. Malcolm X, "Muslim Minister Rips 'Token' Integration," *Muhammad Speaks,* September 15, 1962, reproduced on *Nation of Islam's Women Committed to Preserving the Truth*, August 2006, <http://www.noiwc.org/images/sept151962.pdf> (February 12, 2009).

7. Bruce Perry, *Malcolm X: The Life of a Black Man Who Changed Black America* (Barrytown, N.Y.: Station Hill Press, Inc., 1991), p. 174.

8. Rodnell P. Collins with A. Peter Bailey, *Seventh Child: A Family Memoir of Malcolm X* (Seacaucus, N.J.: Birch Lane Press, 1998), pp. 110–111.

9. Ibid., p. 111.

10. Fidel Castro, "The Case of Cuba Is the Case of All Underdeveloped Countries," September 26, 1960, reprinted on *Hartford Web Publishing,* January 18, 1997, <http://www.hartford-hwp.com/archives/43b/134.html> (March 12, 2009).

11. Clayborne Carson, *Malcolm X: The FBI File* (New York: Carroll and Graf, 1991), p. 198.

12. Perry, p. 226.

13. *Malcolm X: Make It Plain* transcript, *PBS.org,* May 19, 2005, <http://www.pbs.org/wgbh/amex/malcolmx/filmmore/pt.html> (February 19, 2009).

14. Ibid.

15. Ibid.

16. David Gallen, *Malcolm X: As They Knew Him* (New York: Carroll and Graf, 1992), p. 105.

17. *Malcolm X: Make It Plain* transcript.

18. Ibid.

19. "Death and Transfiguration," *Time,* March 5, 1965, <http://www.time.com/time/magazine/article/0,9171,839291-3,00.html> (February 12, 2009).

20. Gallen, pp. 179–180.

Chapter 6: A Bitter Split

1. "I Have a Dream: Address at March on Washington," August 28, 1963, reproduced on *MLK Online,* n.d., <http://www.mlkonline.net/dream.html> (February 1, 2009).

2. Bruce Perry, *Malcolm X: The Life of a Black Man Who Changed Black America* (Barrytown, N.Y.: Station Hill Press, Inc., 1991), p. 211.

3. David Gallen, *Malcolm X: As They Knew Him* (New York: Carroll and Graf, 1992), p. 165.

4. *Malcolm X: Make It Plain* transcript, *PBS.org,* May 19, 2005, <http://www.pbs.org/wgbh/amex/malcolmx/filmmore/pt.html> (February 19, 2009).

5. Perry, p. 241.

6. Ibid.

7. Alex Haley and Malcolm X, *The Autobiography of Malcolm X* (New York: Ballantine Books, 1992), p. 307.

8. Ibid., p. 313.

9. A. B. Spellman, "Interview With Malcolm X," *Monthly Review,* vol. 16, no. 1, May 1964, reprinted on *Hartford Web Publishing,* June 21, 2001, <http://www.hartford-hwp.com/archives/45a/388.html> (March 1, 2009).

10. Perry, pp. 341–342.

11. Gallen, p. 71.

12. Ibid., pp. 71–72.

13. Malcolm X, "Speech on the Founding of the O.A.A.U.," June 28, 1964, reproduced on *Thinking Together,* n.d., <http://www.thinkingtogether.org/rcream/archive/Old/S2006/comp/OAAU.pdf> (February 2, 2009).

14. "Death and Transfiguration," *Time,* March 5, 1965, <http://www.time.com/time/magazine/article/0,9171,839291-4,00.html> (February 12, 2009).

15. John Shabazz, "Muslim Minister Writes to Malcolm," *Muhammad Speaks,* July 3, 1964, p. 9, reproduced on *Center for Contemporary Black History* (Columbia University), n.d., <http://www.columbia.edu/cu/ccbh/mxp/images/sourcebook_img_139.jpg> (February 21, 2009).

16. Clayborne Carson, *Malcolm X: The FBI File* (New York: Carroll and Graf, 1991), p. 324.

17. Ibid.

18. Perry, p. 321.

19. Gallen, pp. 172–173.

20. Perry, p. 351.

21. "Malcolm X Barred," *Times* (London), February 10, 1965, p. B-11, reproduced on *Center for Contemporary Black History* (Columbia University), n.d., <http://www.columbia.edu/cu/ccbh/mxp/images/sourcebook_img_161.jpg> (March 10, 2009).

22. Ibid.

23. Haley and Malcolm X, p. 385.

Chapter 7: A Violent Death

1. Russell J. Rickford, *Betty Shabazz: A Remarkable Story of Survival and Faith Before and After Malcolm X* (Naperville, Ill.: Sourcebooks, Inc., 2003), p. 223.

2. "Malcolm Accuses Muslims of Blaze; They Point to Him," *New York Times,* February 16, 1965, reproduced on *Center for Contemporary Black History* (Columbia University), n.d., <http://www.columbia.edu/cu/ccbh/mxp/images/sourcebook_img_163.jpg> (March 12, 2009).

3. Ibid.

4. "Malcolm X Denies He Is Bomber," *Amsterdam News,* February 20, 1965, reproduced on *Center for Contemporary Black History* (Columbia University), n.d., <http://www.columbia.edu/cu/ccbh/mxp/images/sourcebook_img_165.jpg> (February 21, 2009).

5. Ibid.

6. David Gallen, *Malcolm X: As They Knew Him* (New York: Carroll and Graf, 1992), p. 90.

7. Clayborne Carson, *Malcolm X: The FBI File* (New York: Carroll and Graf, 1991), p. 357.

8. Rickford, pp. 225–226.

9. Alex Haley and Malcolm X, *The Autobiography of Malcolm X* (New York: Ballantine Books, 1992), p. 438.

10. Rickford, p. 228.

11. Ibid., p. 229.

12. Ibid.

13. Peter Kihss, "Malcolm X Shot to Death at Rally Here," *New York Times,* February 22, 1965, reproduced on *Center for Contemporary Black History* (Columbia University), n.d., <http://www.columbia.edu/cu/ccbh/mxp/images/sourcebook_img_169.jpg> (March 12, 2009).

14. Haley and Malcolm X, p. 386.

15. Gallen, p. 177.

16. Kihss, <http://www.columbia.edu/cu/ccbh/mxp/images/sourcebook_img_167.jpg>.

17. Ibid.

18. Ibid.

19. Michael Friedly, *Malcolm X: The Assassination* (New York: Carrol and Graf, 1992), p. 26.

20. Ibid., p. 22.

21. Ibid., p. 49.

Chapter 8: "Sincere" Legacy

1. Russell J. Rickford, *Betty Shabazz: A Remarkable Story of Survival and Faith Before and After Malcolm X* (Naperville, Ill.: Sourcebooks, Inc., 2003), p. 322.
2. Michael Friedly, *Malcolm X: The Assassination* (New York: Carrol and Graf, 1992), p. 85.
3. David Gallen, *Malcolm X: As They Knew Him* (New York: Carroll and Graf, 1992) p. 177.

Further Reading

Benson, Michael. *Malcolm X*. Minneapolis, Minn.: Lerner Classroom, 2005.

Bourcier, Cammy S. *Malcolm X*. Philadelphia: Mason Crest Publishers, 2008.

Freedman, Russell. *Freedom Walkers: The Story of the Montgomery Bus Boycott*. New York: Holiday House, 2006.

Skog, Jason. *The Civil Rights Act of 1964*. Minneapolis, Minn.: Compass Point Books, 2007.

Internet Addresses

Malcolm X Official Site
<http://www.malcolmx.com>

The Civil Rights Movement
<http://www.cnn.com/EVENTS/1997/mlk/links.html>

African American Odyssey: A Quest for Full Citizenship
<http://memory.loc.gov/ammem/aaohtml/exhibit/
aointro.html>

Index